TOWER OF LONDON TRAVEL GUIDE 2024

THE HISTORIC JOURNEY THROUGH THE TOWER OF LONDON

SAM OXFORD

Copyright © 2024 by Sam Oxford. All rights reserved.

No part of this book may be reproduced or transmitted in any form or by any means, electronic or mechanical, including photocopying, recording, or by any information storage and retrieval system, without written permission from the author, except for the inclusion of brief quotations in a review.

TABLE OF CONTENT

INTRODUCTION
1.1 WELCOME NOTE
1.2 OVERVIEW OF THE TOWER OF LONDON
1.3 HISTORICAL SIGNIFICANCE
1.4 LOCATION AND ACCESSIBILITY

HISTORY
2.1 EARLY ORIGINS
2.2 NORMAN CONQUEST AND EXPANSION
2.3 USE AS A ROYAL PALACE
2.4 USE AS A PRISON
2.5 MILITARY FORTIFICATION AND ARMORY
2.6 PRESENT-DAY FUNCTION

ARCHITECTURE AND LAYOUT
3.1 THE WHITE TOWER
3.2 TOWERS AND WALLS
3.3 THE INNER WARD
3.4 THE OUTER WARD
3.5 CROWN JEWELS EXHIBITION

KEY ATTRACTION AND HIGHLIGHTS OF THE TOWER OF LONDON
4.1 THE WHITE TOWER, ROYAL ARMORIES AND MUSEUM
4.2 CROWN JEWELS: THE JEWEL HOUSE

4.3 TOWER GREEN: EXECUTION SITE
4.4 MEDIEVAL PALACE: THE WAKEFIELD TOWER AND ST THOMAS TOWER
4.5 THE YEOMAN WARDERS (BEEFEATERS)
4.6 THE RAVENS OF THE TOWER

GUIDED TOURS AND VISITOR EXPERIENCE
5.1 OPENING HOURS AND ADMISSION
5.2 BEEFEATER-LED TOURS
5.3 AUDIO GUIDES AND MULTIMEDIA EXHIBIT
5.4 TOWER BRIDGE EXHIBITION

5.5 SPECIAL EVENTS AND REENACTMENTS

PRACTICAL INFORMATION FOR VISITORS
6.1 GETTING TO THE TOWER OF LONDON
6.2 TICKETS AND ADMISSION PRICES
6.3 VISITOR FACILITIES
6.4 ACCESSIBILITY INFORMATION
6.5 PHOTOGRAPHY AND FILMING POLICIES

NEARBY ATTRACTIONS AND POINT OF INTEREST
7.1. TOWER BRIDGE
7.2. HMS BELTFAST

7.3 ST. KATHARINE DOCKS
7.4 THE SHARD
7.5 SKY GARDEN

PREPARING FOR YOUR TRIP
8.1 BEST TIME TO VISIT
8.2 PREPARING FOR YOUR VISIT
8.3 RECOMMENDED ITINERARY
8.4 SAFETY AND SECURITY GUIDELINES
8.5 SOUVENIRS AND GIFT SHOPS

TOWER OF LONDON IN POP CULTURE
9.1 LITERATURE AND FILM REFERENCES

9.2 FAMOUS EVENTS AND LEGENDS
9.3 RECENT CULTURAL SIGNIFICANCE

CONCLUSION

INTRODUCTION

1.1 WELCOME NOTE

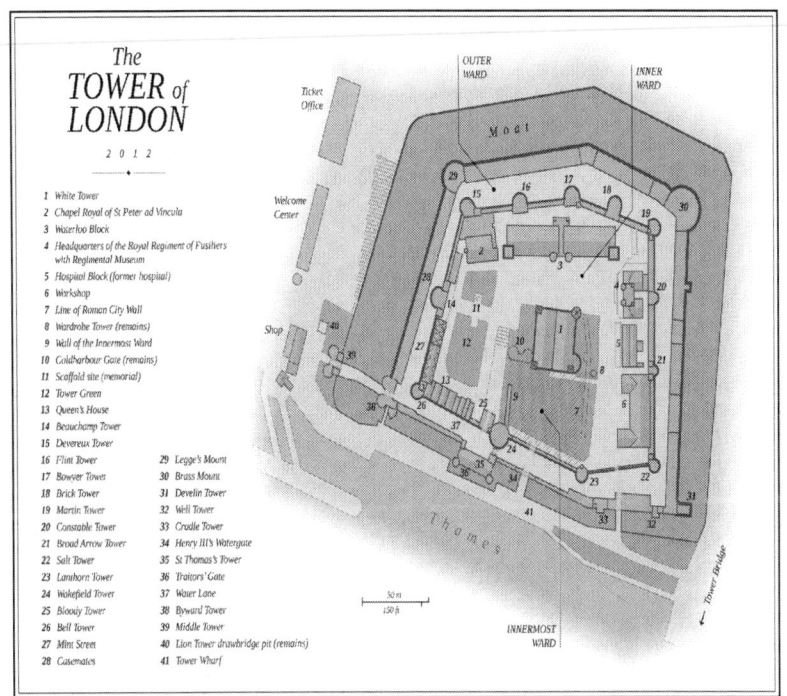

Dear Esteemed Travelers,

Embarking on a journey to the Tower of London is not merely a visit; it is a step back in time, a plunge into history's embrace, and an encounter with the majestic legacy that has withstood centuries. As you cross the threshold of this iconic fortress, prepare to be transported to an era of regal grandeur, political intrigue, and tales that echo through the hallowed halls.

A Tapestry of History Unraveled:

Within these ancient walls, history unfolds like a living tapestry. Imagine the whispers of royal secrets in the chambers of kings and queens, the clinking of armor in the White Tower, and the haunting echoes of the infamous Bloody Tower. Each stone of the Tower of London has witnessed the unfolding drama of power, betrayal, and resilience.

The Crown Jewels' Dazzling Spectacle:

Behold the Crown Jewels, the epitome of opulence and magnificence. Marvel at the sparkle of diamonds, the gleam of gold, and the rich history encapsulated in each gem. The Crown Jewels not only symbolize the monarchy's splendor but also bear witness to the resilience of a nation.

Guardians of Legend: The Yeomen Warders:

Meet the Yeomen Warders, the ceremonial guardians who have stood watch over the Tower for centuries. Their vibrant uniforms and captivating tales add a human touch to the stone façade, offering a glimpse into the daily lives of those who have protected this historic fortress.

13

Ravens: Sentinels of Fate:

Keep an eye out for the Tower's mystical residents – the ravens. Legend has it that the fate of the kingdom is tied to these ebony-feathered guardians. Their presence adds an air of mystery and enchantment, making your journey even more enthralling.

14

Interactive Exhibits: Engaging History:

Step into the interactive exhibits that breathe life into the past. Explore the medieval architecture, handle replica armor, and immerse yourself in the vivid storytelling that transcends time. The Tower of London invites you not only to witness history but to actively participate in its unraveling.

Unforgettable Views of London:

Ascend the battlements and savor panoramic views of the Thames and the city beyond. The juxtaposition of ancient fortifications against the modern skyline creates a visual spectacle that bridges the gap between centuries, offering a unique perspective on London's evolution.

Your Journey Begins:

As you embark on this extraordinary journey through the Tower of London, let the echoes of the past resonate within you. Feel the weight of history, the allure of the unknown, and the sheer grandiosity of this living monument. Your presence here is not just as a traveler; it is as a custodian of a shared history, a witness to the stories etched into these stones.

May your visit to the Tower of London be an immersive and unforgettable experience, as you become part of the living history that breathes within its walls.

Welcome, intrepid traveler, to a realm where the past converges with the present, and every step is a dance with the echoes of royalty and rebellion.

Yours in History's Embrace,

Sam Oxford
Your Tower Guide

1.2 OVERVIEW OF THE TOWER OF LONDON

The Tower of London, also known as Her Majesty's Royal Palace and Fortress of the Tower of London, is a historic castle located on the north bank of the River Thames in central London, England. It has a rich and fascinating history spanning over 900 years and has played a significant role in the development of the city and the nation.

Construction of the Tower of London began in 1078 under the orders of William the Conqueror, the first Norman king of England. The original purpose of the tower was to act as a royal residence and a symbol of power and authority. Over the centuries, it underwent several expansions and modifications under the reign of subsequent monarchs, including Henry III, Edward I, and Richard the Lionheart.

One of the tower's most famous features is the White Tower, which gives the entire complex its name. The White Tower is a massive stone keep that stands at the heart of the fortress. It was initially built as a symbol of royal might and as a defensive structure. The tower's architecture is a mix of Norman and Romanesque styles, characterized by its thick walls, small windows, and sturdy appearance.

Throughout its history, the Tower of London has served various functions. It has been used as a royal palace, a treasury, a menagerie, and most notably, a prison. The tower gained a reputation as a place of imprisonment and execution, with several high-profile individuals being held captive within its walls. Notable prisoners include Anne Boleyn, Sir Walter Raleigh, and Guy Fawkes.

Perhaps the most iconic role of the Tower of London was as a prison for traitors and a site of public execution. The tower's most famous execution site, known as the Tower Hill, witnessed the beheading of many notable figures, including three English queens: Anne Boleyn, Catherine Howard, and Lady Jane Grey.

Another integral part of the Tower of London's

history is the Crown Jewels. Since the 14th century, the tower has been home to the Crown Jewels of England, which include the Imperial State Crown, the Sovereign's Sceptre, and the famous Koh-i-Noor diamond. The Crown Jewels are on public display and attract millions of visitors each year.

Today, the Tower of London is a UNESCO World Heritage Site and a major tourist attraction. Visitors can explore the castle's numerous buildings, including the White Tower, the Medieval Palace, and the Royal Chapel of St. Peter ad Vincula. The Yeoman Warders, also known as Beefeaters, offer guided tours that provide insights into the tower's history, legends, and tales of intrigue.

In addition to its historical significance, the Tower of London is also known for its ravens. According to legend, if the ravens ever leave the tower, the kingdom will fall. As a result, a group of ravens is always kept at the tower and cared for by the Yeoman Warders.

The Tower of London stands as a symbol of England's rich and complex history. From its origins as a medieval fortress to its role as a royal residence, a prison, and a treasury, the tower has witnessed pivotal moments in the nation's past. Today, it continues to captivate visitors with its architectural grandeur, historical artifacts, and intriguing stories, making it a must-visit destination for anyone interested in England's fascinating past.

1.3 HISTORICAL SIGNIFICANCE

The Tower of London is an iconic landmark situated in the heart of London, England, along the banks of the River Thames. With a rich and storied history spanning over 900 years, the Tower of London has served numerous roles throughout its existence, including a royal palace, a prison, an armory, a treasury, and even a menagerie.

The Tower's origins can be traced back to the reign of William the Conqueror, who ordered its construction in 1078 as a symbol of his power and a fortress to protect the newly conquered city of London. The initial structure, known as the White Tower, was a massive stone keep with walls over 15 feet thick. Over the centuries, additional buildings and fortifications were added, expanding the complex into a formidable stronghold.

One of the Tower of London's most famous functions was as a prison and a place of execution. The tower's history is tinged with tales of political intrigue, power struggles, and bloody executions. Many notable figures were imprisoned within its walls, including Anne Boleyn, the second wife of Henry VIII, who was accused of adultery and treason and met her tragic end on the executioner's block in 1536.

The Tower also gained a notorious reputation as a place of torture and interrogation during the medieval period. The infamous torture chambers within its walls witnessed the torment of many prisoners accused of treason or heresy. Instruments such as the rack, the Scavenger's Daughter, and the Iron Maiden were employed to extract confessions or punish the accused.

Another fascinating aspect of the Tower's history is its function as an armory and treasury. The White Tower housed an extensive collection of weapons, armor, and military equipment, highlighting the importance of the Tower as a strategic stronghold. The Crown Jewels of England, including the magnificent crowns, scepters, and orbs used in royal ceremonies, are also kept in the Tower's Jewel House, where they are displayed to the public.

Throughout the centuries, the Tower of London served as a symbol of royal authority, and its impressive architecture and imposing presence added to its mystique. It remained a working royal palace until the 17th century, when the monarchs began to favor other residences. However, the Tower has continued to play a ceremonial role in royal events, such as the coronation of monarchs and the occasional confinement of prisoners of special importance.

In addition to its historical significance, the Tower of London has become a popular tourist attraction and is a UNESCO World Heritage site. Visitors can explore its various buildings, walk along its ancient walls, and witness the iconic Yeoman Warders, also known as the "Beefeaters," who serve as guides and guardians of the Tower.

The Tower of London stands as a testament to the turbulent and eventful history of England. It has witnessed the rise and fall of kings and queens, the dramas of political intrigue, and the dark chapters of human suffering. Today, it serves as a reminder of the nation's heritage and a window into the past, attracting millions of visitors each year who are captivated by its historical significance and architectural grandeur.

1.4 LOCATION AND ACCESSIBILITY

The Tower of London, located in the heart of London, England, is a historic castle complex that has played a significant role in the city's rich history. Situated on the north bank of the River Thames, in the borough of Tower Hamlets, the Tower of London is one of the most iconic landmarks in the city and a popular tourist destination. Its central location makes it easily accessible for both locals and visitors from around the world.

The Tower of London's address is Tower Hill, London EC3N 4AB, United Kingdom. It stands on the eastern edge of the City of London, close to other famous landmarks such as the Tower Bridge, HMS Belfast, and the Shard. The tower's strategic location has made it an important fortification and stronghold since its construction in the 11th century.

Accessibility to the Tower of London is excellent, with various transportation options available. Visitors can easily reach the site using public transportation, including buses, trains, and the London Underground (also known as the Tube). The nearest Tube station to the Tower is Tower Hill station, which is served by the

District and Circle lines. It is located just a short walk away, making it a convenient choice for those traveling within London.

Additionally, several bus routes pass near the Tower of London, making it accessible from different parts of the city. The Tower Gateway DLR (Docklands Light Railway) station is also nearby, providing connections to various destinations in East London.

For those who prefer to explore London by river, the Tower of London has its own pier, appropriately named Tower Pier. River buses operated by Thames Clippers serve this pier, offering a scenic and unique way to reach the Tower while enjoying breathtaking views of the city's waterfront.

Visitors arriving by car can also reach the Tower of London, but it's important to note that parking in the area can be challenging due to high demand and limited space. It is advisable to use public transportation or nearby parking facilities and walk to the Tower.

Once at the Tower of London, visitors can explore its various attractions, including the White Tower, the oldest part of the complex, which houses the Royal Armouries collection. The Crown Jewels, a remarkable display of royal regalia, are also on exhibit and are a major highlight for many visitors. The tower is also renowned for its iconic Yeoman Warders, commonly known as Beefeaters, who provide guided tours and share captivating stories from the tower's history.

The Tower of London's central location and excellent accessibility via public transportation make it a must-visit destination for both locals and tourists. Its address in Tower Hill, London, places it within easy reach of multiple transport options, including the Tube, buses, trains, and river services. Whether you're interested in history, architecture, or simply want to experience the grandeur of this iconic landmark, the Tower of London offers a captivating and accessible experience for all.

2.0 HISTORY

2.1 EARLY ORIGINS:

London, has a rich and fascinating history that stretches back over a millennium. Its early origins are rooted in the eleventh century, and the Tower has since served various purposes throughout its existence, ranging from a royal palace to a notorious prison and a treasury. Let's delve into the early origin of this iconic landmark.

Construction of the Tower of London began in the late 1060s under the orders of William the Conqueror, the Duke of Normandy who had successfully invaded England in 1066 and became its first Norman King. William wanted to establish a symbol of his power and dominance over the newly conquered city of London, as well as to provide a fortress that would serve as a stronghold for defense and control.

The Tower was built as a stone fortress, encircled by a massive defensive wall with numerous towers. Its strategic location on the River Thames ensured control over river traffic and secured a key entry point into the city. The original structure, known as the White Tower, was completed around 1100. It consisted of four stories and featured thick walls, imposing turrets, and a keep that served as the residence of the king.

During the early medieval period, the Tower of London underwent significant expansions and modifications. Additional fortifications were constructed, including the inner curtain wall, which created an inner ward known as the Inner Bailey. Several towers, such as the Wakefield Tower and the Lanthorn Tower, were added to enhance the defenses and provide additional accommodations.

The Tower's primary function as a royal palace and a symbol of Norman authority continued during the reign of subsequent English monarchs. It served as a residence for kings and queens, a venue for royal ceremonies and feasts, and a place to display wealth and power. Notable monarchs, including Henry III, Edward I, and Edward III, made substantial additions to the Tower complex, expanding the living quarters and adding chapels and other structures.

Over time, the Tower of London also began to serve a secondary role as a prison. Its reputation as a place of incarceration began during the reign of Henry III in the thirteenth century. By the fourteenth century, the Tower was commonly used to hold high-profile prisoners, including political rivals, traitors, and members of the nobility. Some of the notable figures imprisoned within its walls include Anne Boleyn, Sir Walter Raleigh, and Guy Fawkes.

Another function of the Tower was that of a treasury and a secure storage facility for valuable items, including the Crown Jewels. The Jewel House was established within the Tower's walls in the late thirteenth century, and it remains the home of the Crown Jewels to this day, attracting millions of visitors each year.

The Tower of London continued to evolve throughout the centuries, with further expansions and modifications undertaken by subsequent monarchs. However, its importance as a royal residence gradually diminished, and by the seventeenth century, it was primarily used as a military garrison and an arsenal.

Despite its changing roles, the Tower of London remained a symbol of royal authority and power throughout English history. It also played a significant role in shaping the city of London itself. The Tower's presence contributed to the development of the surrounding area, and it became a focal point for trade, commerce, and cultural activities.

Today, the Tower of London stands as a UNESCO World Heritage Site and one of the most popular tourist attractions in the United Kingdom. Its early origins as a Norman fortress, palace, prison, and treasury have left an indelible mark on British history, making it a site of immense historical and cultural significance.

2.2 NORMAN CONQUEST AND EXPANSION:

The Norman Conquest and the Tower of London hold significant historical importance in the development of England. The conquest, led by William the Conqueror in 1066, marked the beginning of Norman rule in England and the establishment of the iconic Tower of London as a symbol of power, defense, and control.

The Norman Conquest itself was a pivotal event in English history. It occurred when William, the Duke of Normandy, invaded England and defeated King Harold II at the Battle of Hastings on October 14, 1066. This victory established William as the new King of England and initiated the Norman dynasty.

One of the key aspects of William's reign was his focus on solidifying his authority and control over the newly conquered territory. To achieve this, he initiated various construction projects, including the construction of the Tower of London. The Tower served multiple purposes, serving as a royal residence, a fortress, a symbol of power, and a deterrent against rebellions.

The Tower of London was initially built as a timber fortification by William the Conqueror, shortly after his victory at Hastings. It was strategically located on the eastern edge of the city, near the River Thames, allowing it to control access to the capital. The original structure was known as the White Tower, owing to the white limestone used in its construction.

Over time, subsequent monarchs expanded and strengthened the Tower. Henry II, who reigned from 1154 to 1189, added curtain walls and other defensive structures, transforming it into a formidable fortress. The Tower's expansion continued under the reigns of Richard the Lionheart and King John. King John, in particular, added the outer curtain walls, creating the concentric design that characterizes the Tower of London to this day.

The Tower's expansion was not solely focused on defense. It also served as a royal residence, providing accommodation for kings, queens, and other members of the royal family. The tower complex included various buildings such as the Royal Palace, the White Tower, the Wakefield Tower, the St. Thomas's Tower, and the Bloody Tower. These structures housed royal apartments, chapels, and other amenities befitting the monarchy.

Additionally, the Tower of London played a significant role in the governance of England. It served as a royal mint, where coins were produced, and as a treasury, storing valuable items such as the Crown Jewels. It was also used as a prison, holding notable prisoners over the centuries, including high-ranking nobles, political figures, and even monarchs. Famous prisoners of the Tower include Anne Boleyn, Sir Walter Raleigh, and Guy Fawkes.

The Tower of London underwent further expansion and modification in the later medieval and Tudor periods. Edward I reinforced the Tower's defenses, adding the outer ward and the Beauchamp Tower. The Tudor monarchs, notably Henry VIII and Elizabeth I, utilized the Tower as a symbol of their power and authority. They conducted lavish ceremonies, held royal feasts, and displayed their wealth and prestige within its walls.

As time went on, the Tower of London's role as a royal residence diminished, and its significance shifted more towards ceremonial and historical purposes. Today, the Tower stands as a popular tourist attraction and a UNESCO World Heritage site. It houses the Crown Jewels, the Royal Armories, and various exhibits that showcase its rich history.

The Norman Conquest and the expansion of the Tower of London are intertwined in English history. The conquest marked the beginning of Norman rule and initiated a period of significant political, cultural, and architectural changes. The Tower of London, as a symbol of Norman power, underwent expansion and transformation throughout the centuries, reflecting the evolving needs of the monarchy and serving as a testament to England's rich heritage.

2.3 USE AS A ROYAL PALACE

The Tower of London, located in the heart of the city of London, has a rich and fascinating history that stretches back nearly a millennium. While it is most commonly known as a historic fortress and prison, the Tower of London also served as a royal palace for various periods throughout its existence. Its dual function as a palace and a fortress made it a unique and significant structure in the context of British history.

The origins of the Tower of London as a royal residence can be traced back to the reign of William the Conqueror, who ordered its construction in 1078. Initially built as a symbol of Norman power and authority, the Tower quickly became a vital stronghold in London's defense system. However, it wasn't until the reign of Henry III in the 13th century that the Tower began to be used as a royal palace.

Under Henry III and subsequent monarchs, the Tower underwent significant expansions and renovations to accommodate the needs of the royal family. Palatial apartments were constructed, including the sumptuous St. Thomas's Tower and the luxurious Wakefield Tower. These structures housed various members of the royal family, including kings, queens, and their retinues. The Tower became a place of residence, entertainment, and administration for the monarchy.

During the medieval period, the Tower of London was a vibrant center of courtly life and pageantry. It played host to grand ceremonies, banquets, and celebrations, reflecting the opulence and grandeur of the monarchy. The royal apartments within the Tower were adorned with lavish decorations, tapestries, and artwork, creating a regal ambiance befitting a royal residence.

Notable monarchs who made use of the Tower of London as a palace include Richard II, who extensively expanded the royal apartments, and Henry VIII, who spent significant periods of his reign within its walls. Henry VIII used the Tower as a base for his courtly activities, and he celebrated his marriages to Anne Boleyn and Jane Seymour within its confines. The Tower of London was also the birthplace of several royal children, including Edward V and Elizabeth I.

Despite its grandeur as a royal palace, the Tower of London remained primarily a fortress and a symbol of royal authority. Its location on the banks of the River Thames and its strategic position within the city walls made it a formidable stronghold. The Tower's famous White Tower, the central keep, served as a symbol of royal power and was an imposing presence on the London skyline.

Over the centuries, the Tower of London gradually lost its status as a royal residence. As the monarchy's preferences shifted toward more comfortable and modern palaces, such as Hampton Court and St. James's Palace, the

Tower became predominantly associated with imprisonment and punishment. Notable prisoners, including Sir Walter Raleigh, Anne Boleyn, and Sir Thomas More, were held within its walls, adding to its notorious reputation.

Despite this transition, the Tower of London retained its ceremonial and symbolic importance for the monarchy. The Crown Jewels, including the iconic Imperial State Crown, are still stored and displayed within the Tower, emphasizing its enduring connection to royal authority and heritage.

Today, the Tower of London stands as a UNESCO World Heritage site and one of London's most popular tourist attractions. It serves as a museum and a monument to Britain's rich history, showcasing its dual roles as a royal palace and a fortress. Visitors can explore the royal apartments, marvel at the Crown Jewels, and delve into the stories of the Tower's famous prisoners. The Tower's historical significance as a royal palace continues to captivate and inspire people from around the world.

The Tower of London is widely known for its role as a fortress and a prison, it also served as a royal palace for various periods throughout history. From its origins as a symbol of Norman power and authority to its transformation into a grand residence for the monarchy, the Tower of London played a significant role in the lives of British kings and queens.

The Tower's status as a royal palace was not only a reflection of the monarchy's need for a fortified stronghold but also a symbol of their power and prestige. Its imposing architecture, fortified walls, and strategic location along the River Thames made it an ideal residence for the monarchs, offering both security and a commanding presence within the city.

The royal apartments within the Tower were designed to provide comfort and luxury to the royal residents. These apartments boasted grand chambers, private chapels, and even gardens for leisurely strolls. The interiors were adorned with exquisite furnishings, fine tapestries, and ornate decorations, showcasing the wealth and taste of the monarchy. The Tower's royal residents could enjoy the privileges of courtly life within the confines of the fortress, surrounded by opulence and splendor.

Furthermore, the Tower of London as a royal palace served various functions beyond being a residence. It was a center of governance and administration, with the monarch's council meeting within its walls to discuss matters of state. Important ceremonies, such as the investiture of knights and the receiving of foreign dignitaries, took place within the Tower's grand halls, adding to its significance as a royal venue.

The Tower also played a role in the defense and protection of the realm. It housed the Royal Mint, where coins were minted, ensuring the monarch's control over the currency. The fortress was equipped with armories, barracks, and military installations, allowing the monarchy to maintain a strong military presence in the heart of the capital.

However, as the monarchy evolved and the needs of the royal family changed, the Tower of London gradually ceased to serve as a primary royal residence. The Tudor monarchs, in particular, favored other palaces, such as Hampton Court and Greenwich, for their comfort and modern amenities. The Tower's association with imprisonment and execution, particularly during the Tudor period, also contributed to its diminishing appeal as a royal residence.

Nevertheless, the Tower's symbolic importance and historical significance remained intact. The Tower continued to be an integral part of royal ceremonies and traditions. The Yeoman Warders, commonly known as Beefeaters, have guarded the Tower for centuries, upholding its traditions and adding to its mystique. The Crown Jewels, housed within the Tower, symbolize the continuity of royal authority and are displayed to the public, attracting millions of visitors each year.

Today, the Tower of London stands as a living testament to its multifaceted history. It is a captivating blend of fortress, palace, and museum, where visitors can explore the ancient walls, admire the architecture, and learn about the Tower's role in shaping the nation's history. The Tower's unique position as both a royal palace and a symbol of power and imprisonment makes it a remarkable and evocative landmark that continues to captivate the imagination of people from around the world.

The Tower of London's use as a royal palace underscores its historical significance and multifaceted nature. From its origins as a fortress to its transformation into a grand residence, the Tower of London served as a symbol of royal power, a center of courtly life, and a hub of governance. While its role as a royal residence diminished over time, the Tower's enduring symbolic importance and its place in British history make it an iconic landmark that continues to inspire and fascinate visitors.

2.4 USE AS A PRISON:

One of the most well-known aspects of its history is its use as a prison. Throughout the centuries, the Tower has been used to incarcerate a wide range of prisoners, from high-ranking nobles to political opponents and even common criminals. The Tower's reputation as a prison is shrouded in legends, tales of intrigue, and stories of torture and execution.

The Tower's use as a prison can be traced back to its original construction in the 11th century. William the Conqueror, the first Norman king of England, commissioned the Tower's construction in 1066 as a symbol of his power and dominance over the newly conquered kingdom. However, the Tower quickly took on additional roles, including that of a royal residence, treasury, and, importantly, a prison.

During the medieval period, the Tower was primarily used to incarcerate individuals of high social or political status who posed a threat to the reigning monarch or the kingdom itself. One of the most famous early prisoners was Ranulf Flambard, the Bishop of Durham, who became the first recorded prisoner of the Tower in 1100. Flambard had been involved in a rebellion against King William II, and his imprisonment in the Tower set a precedent for the incarceration of powerful figures who opposed the crown.

Over the centuries, the Tower witnessed numerous significant political and religious upheavals, resulting in the imprisonment of various notable figures. During the reign of King Henry VIII, the Tower housed two of his wives, Anne Boleyn and Catherine Howard, both of whom were accused of adultery and treason. Both women met their tragic ends within the Tower's walls, with Anne Boleyn being executed on charges of adultery and conspiracy in 1536 and Catherine Howard suffering the same fate in 1542.

The religious conflicts of the 16th and 17th centuries also led to the imprisonment of religious dissenters and those accused of heresy. Notable examples include Thomas More, the renowned philosopher and Lord Chancellor of England, who was imprisoned in the Tower for refusing to acknowledge Henry VIII as the head of the Church of England. More was ultimately executed in 1535. The Tower also held the future Archbishop of Canterbury, Thomas Cranmer, and the Catholic martyr, St. Thomas More.

During the reign of Queen Elizabeth I, the Tower of London witnessed a significant shift in its use as a prison. While political prisoners were still held within its walls, the Tower began to be increasingly used as a state prison for individuals accused of treason, conspiracy, and espionage. Famous prisoners during this period included Guy Fawkes, who was part of the Gunpowder Plot to assassinate King James I, and Sir Walter Raleigh, the explorer and writer who was accused of involvement in a conspiracy against the queen.

The Tower's use as a prison continued well into the 19th and 20th centuries, albeit with decreasing frequency. The last known prisoner to be held in the Tower was the Nazi Rudolf Hess, who was captured in Scotland during World War II. He was subsequently held in the Tower from 1941 until 1945 before being transferred to other prisons.

Throughout its history, the Tower of London's reputation as a prison was accompanied by stories of torture, execution, and ghostly apparitions. The Tower's dungeons were infamous for their grim conditions, and prisoners were subjected to various forms of torture to extract confessions or information. The Tower's most iconic execution site, Tower Hill, witnessed the beheading of numerous individuals, both inside and outside the Tower's walls.

Today, the Tower of London stands as a historic site and a popular tourist attraction. While it no longer functions as a prison, its dark and compelling past as a place of imprisonment still lingers in its ancient walls. The Tower's role as a prison has left an indelible mark on its architecture and atmosphere, evoking a sense of intrigue and foreboding.

Visitors to the Tower of London can explore the very cells and chambers where prisoners were once held captive. The Beauchamp Tower, for example, bears the etchings and graffiti of former prisoners who sought solace in leaving their mark on the stone walls. These inscriptions serve as poignant reminders of the individuals who endured confinement within the Tower's confines.

The Tower's reputation as a place of torture and execution is also manifested in the infamous Traitor's Gate. This water gate provided a chilling entrance for those prisoners who arrived at the Tower by river. The sight of Traitor's Gate, with its dark and imposing presence, undoubtedly struck fear into the hearts of those unfortunate enough to pass through its threshold.

The Tower's role as a prison extended beyond confinement and punishment. It also served as a symbol of power and a deterrent to potential dissidents. The sight of the Tower looming over the city of London served as a constant reminder of the consequences that awaited those who dared to challenge the monarchy or engage in treasonous activities.

While the Tower of London is known for its high-profile prisoners, it also held numerous lesser-known individuals whose stories are no less fascinating. From religious reformers to accused witches, the Tower housed a diverse array of individuals who found themselves at odds with the political and religious establishments of their time.

It is important to note that not all prisoners held within the Tower's walls were subjected to harsh treatment. Some prisoners of high rank were afforded certain privileges and comforts, often reflecting their social status. However, for many others, the Tower represented a place of unimaginable suffering, where their fates were sealed by the whim of those in power.

The Tower's reputation as a prison is further heightened by the numerous ghostly legends and tales associated with the site. Over the years, stories of apparitions, eerie sounds, and inexplicable phenomena have circulated, adding an air of mystique and haunting to the Tower's history. The ghostly presence of figures such as Anne Boleyn, the Princes in the Tower, and even the ghostly White Lady has become part of the Tower's folklore, captivating the imaginations of visitors and fueling its reputation as one of the most haunted places in England.

The Tower of London's use as a prison spans centuries and is intertwined with the complex tapestry of British history. From the confinement of high-ranking nobles to the incarceration of religious dissenters and common criminals, the Tower's prison walls have witnessed the struggles, conspiracies, and tragedies of individuals who found themselves at odds with the powers that be. Today, the Tower stands as a testament to this dark chapter of history, inviting visitors to explore its storied past and unravel the secrets that lie within its formidable walls

2.5 MILITARY FORTIFICATION AND ARMORY:

The Tower has also served as a prison, treasury, and, most notably, a military fortification and armory. This majestic structure stands as a symbol of power and authority, representing the might of the British monarchy and its military prowess.

MILITARY FORTIFICATION:

The Tower of London was strategically positioned along the River Thames, offering a defensive advantage and controlling access to the city. Its primary purpose was to protect the city from external threats, including foreign invasions and rebellions. Over the centuries, the Tower underwent numerous expansions and enhancements to strengthen its defensive capabilities.

The White Tower, the central keep of the complex, forms the core of the military fortifications. Built by William the Conqueror in the 11th century, it features thick walls, sturdy battlements, and small, narrow windows that allowed for archers to defend the structure effectively. The walls are constructed of Kentish ragstone and reach up to 27.5 meters (90 feet) in height, providing a formidable barrier against attackers.

Additionally, the Tower is surrounded by a curtain wall and several defensive towers, such as the Beauchamp Tower, the Bell Tower, and the Bloody Tower. These structures formed an outer ring of protection, making it challenging for assailants to breach the fortifications. Each tower had its unique defensive features, such as arrow slits, battlements, and machicolations, allowing defenders to rain arrows or boiling liquids on attackers.

The Tower's defenses were further strengthened by the presence of a moat, which surrounded the complex until the 19th century. The moat acted as a physical barrier and an additional line of defense. It was filled with water from the Thames and supplemented by a tidal mill that could control the water level, making it difficult for besiegers to approach the fortress.

ARMORY:

The Tower of London has long been renowned as a significant armory and repository of royal treasures. It served as a secure storage facility for weapons, armor, and other military equipment crucial for defending the kingdom. The armory housed an impressive collection of arms and armor, ranging from medieval times to the modern era.

Inside the White Tower, the Royal Armories Museum showcases a vast array of historical weaponry, including swords, polearms, crossbows, and firearms. Visitors can marvel at the intricate craftsmanship of suits of armor worn by knights, reflecting the styles and technologies of different eras. The collection offers a unique glimpse into the evolution of military technology and the artistry of armorers throughout history.

One of the most iconic features of the Tower's armory is the Line of Kings, a display of wooden horse-mounted figures wearing armor. The Line of Kings was established in the 17th century and has since evolved to reflect changing fashions and historical accuracy. It represents a visual timeline of the monarchy's military history and was an early precursor to modern museum exhibitions.

The Tower's armory also stored valuable royal regalia and treasures. The Jewel House, located in the Waterloo Block, protects the Crown Jewels of the United Kingdom. This collection includes crowns, scepters, orbs, and other ceremonial items that symbolize the monarchy's power and authority.

The Tower of London's armory and military fortifications have witnessed countless historical events, from political struggles to acts of rebellion. Today, it stands not only as a popular tourist attraction but also as a testament to the rich military heritage of the United Kingdom. Its fortifications and armory continue to inspire awe and fascination, providing a tangible link to the country's past and the legacy of its military might.

2.6 PRESENT-DAY FUNCTION:

The Tower of London, located in the heart of the city of London, is an iconic and historic landmark that has played a significant role in the history and governance of England. While it is known for its rich and often turbulent past, the Tower of London serves various functions in the present day, encompassing both historical preservation and tourism.

HISTORICAL SITE AND MUSEUM:
The Tower of London serves as a living testament to England's history. It is a designated UNESCO World Heritage Site and attracts millions of visitors each year. As a museum, it houses a vast collection of artifacts, artworks, and exhibits that chronicle the Tower's past and its significance in shaping English history. Visitors can explore various areas within the Tower, including the White Tower, Medieval

Palace, Crown Jewels, and the infamous Tower Green.

HOME OF THE CROWN JEWELS:
One of the Tower of London's most famous attractions is the Jewel House, which houses the Crown Jewels of the British monarchy. This collection includes the regalia and precious gems used in the coronations of English and British monarchs throughout history. Visitors can view the Crown Jewels, including crowns, scepters, orbs, and ceremonial swords, and learn about their historical and cultural significance.

HISTORIC ROYAL PALACE:
The Tower of London is an official royal palace and remains a residence of the reigning monarch of England. While it is no longer a primary residence, certain areas within the Tower, such as the Wakefield Tower and the Queen's House, are used for ceremonial purposes. The Yeoman Warders, also known as the Beefeaters, who guard the Tower, are active and retired military personnel who reside within the complex.

TOURIST ATTRACTION:

As one of the most visited landmarks in the United Kingdom, the Tower of London is a significant tourist attraction. Its historical importance, captivating architecture, and cultural significance draw visitors from around the world. Guided tours, interactive exhibits, and live demonstrations by the Yeoman Warders provide visitors with an immersive experience, offering insights into the Tower's fascinating history, including its use as a fortress, royal palace, prison, and treasury.

CULTURAL EVENTS AND EXHIBITIONS:

The Tower of London hosts various cultural events and exhibitions throughout the year, further enriching its role in contemporary society. These events include historical reenactments, concerts, art exhibitions, and special displays that celebrate English heritage. The Tower also plays a significant role in national ceremonies and events, such as the

Ceremony of the Keys, which is a nightly ritual dating back over 700 years.

CONSERVATION AND PRESERVATION:
Preserving the Tower's historical buildings, artifacts, and infrastructure is a crucial function of the Tower of London. A dedicated team of conservation experts and historians work tirelessly to maintain and protect the structures and objects within the complex. This includes regular maintenance, restoration projects, and research to ensure the continued preservation of the Tower's heritage for future generations.

EDUCATION AND RESEARCH:
The Tower of London serves as an educational resource, providing opportunities for learning and research. It offers educational programs and workshops designed for schools, universities, and scholars, allowing them to delve deeper into the Tower's historical significance. Researchers have access to the extensive archives and collections, contributing to a better understanding of England's past.

SYMBOL OF BRITISH IDENTITY:

The Tower of London remains a powerful symbol of British identity, representing the monarchy, history, and resilience of the nation. Its iconic silhouette against the London skyline is instantly recognizable and serves as a testament to the country's rich cultural heritage.

The Tower of London fulfills a multitude of functions in the present day. It serves as a historical site, museum, and royal palace, housing the Crown Jewels and preserving England's rich heritage. Simultaneously, it is a tourist attraction, hosting cultural events and exhibitions, and offering educational and research opportunities. Additionally, the Tower of London symbolizes British identity and serves as a reminder of the country's history and resilience.

The Tower's role as a tourist attraction cannot be overstated. Its historical significance, architectural grandeur, and captivating stories attract millions of visitors each year. Tourists have the opportunity to explore the Tower's various sections, guided by expert Yeoman Warders who share fascinating tales and insights into its past. Visitors can witness live demonstrations of historical events, such as medieval weapon displays or the changing of the guards, further enhancing the immersive experience.

Furthermore, the Tower of London plays host to a range of cultural events and exhibitions. These events showcase different aspects of English history and culture, attracting both locals and international visitors. Historical reenactments bring the Tower's past to life, offering a glimpse into the dramatic events that unfolded within its walls. Concerts and art exhibitions provide a contemporary touch to the historic setting, creating a unique blend of tradition and modernity.

Education and research are also integral to the Tower of London's present-day function. The

Tower offers educational programs tailored for students of all ages, providing them with a deeper understanding of its historical context. Schools and universities can arrange visits that combine guided tours with interactive workshops, enabling students to engage with history in a tangible and meaningful way. The Tower's archives and collections are valuable resources for researchers and scholars, offering a wealth of primary materials for historical study and exploration.

In addition to its cultural and educational roles, the Tower of London continues to preserve and conserve its historic structures and artifacts. Dedicated teams of conservation experts work diligently to ensure the longevity of the Tower's buildings, safeguarding them for future generations. Restoration projects, ongoing maintenance, and scientific research contribute to the preservation of the Tower's architectural integrity and historical authenticity.

Lastly, the Tower of London remains an enduring symbol of British identity. Its iconic image and rich history evoke a sense of national pride, reminding both the British people and visitors from around the world of the country's storied past. The Tower's association with the monarchy and its role as a bastion of power and authority reinforces its significance as a symbol of England's heritage and enduring cultural legacy.

The Tower of London is a multifaceted institution that serves numerous functions in the present day. It is a historical site, museum, royal palace, tourist attraction, cultural venue, educational resource, research center, and a symbol of British identity. With its blend of history, preservation, tourism, and cultural engagement, the Tower of London continues to captivate and inspire people from all walks of life, ensuring that its legacy endures well into the future.

3.0 ARCHITECTURE AND LAYOUT

3.1 THE WHITE TOWER:

The White Tower stands as the most prominent and iconic structure within the Tower of London complex. It is a massive stone keep situated on the northern bank of the River Thames in central London, England. The tower's architecture is a remarkable example of Norman military and royal architecture, reflecting its construction during the late 11th century.

The White Tower has a rectangular plan, measuring approximately 36 meters (118 feet) by 32 meters (105 feet). It rises to a height of around 27 meters (90 feet), comprising three main stories with an additional storey above. The tower is constructed using Kentish ragstone, which lends it a distinctive white appearance and gives rise to its name.

The exterior of the White Tower features four corner turrets, each with a round or octagonal shape. These turrets, along with the crenellated parapets, contribute to the tower's imposing and fortified appearance. The entrance is situated on the south side and is accessed through a grand Norman archway, which leads into the spacious interior courtyard.

Inside the White Tower, visitors can explore various levels and rooms, including the basement, ground floor, first floor, and second floor. The ground floor houses the famous Chapel of St. John, an exquisite example of Romanesque architecture, adorned with arches, columns, and decorative stonework. This chapel served as a place of worship for the royal court during the medieval period.

The first floor of the White Tower accommodates the magnificent Medieval Palace, which was once a residence for royalty. The palace rooms showcase the historical living quarters of kings and queens, with elaborately decorated chambers, fireplaces, and intricate wooden ceilings. The second floor comprises the Council Chamber, a space where important meetings and discussions were held.

3.2 TOWERS AND WALLS:

Surrounding the White Tower, a series of towers and walls form a defensive fortification, providing additional layers of security and creating distinct areas within the Tower of London complex. These towers and walls were constructed at different times throughout history, resulting in a diverse architectural ensemble.

The towers within the Tower of London complex include the Beauchamp Tower, Bell Tower, Bloody Tower, Brick Tower, Broad Arrow Tower, Constable Tower, Cradle Tower, Devereux Tower, Flint Tower, Lanthorn Tower, Martin Tower, Middle Tower, St. Thomas's Tower, Salt Tower, and Wakefield Tower, among others.

Each tower exhibits unique architectural features and served specific functions. For instance, the Bell Tower housed the royal treasury, while the Bloody Tower gained infamy for its association with the imprisonment and possible murder of the Princes in the Tower during the reign of Richard III. Many of these towers were used as accommodation for prisoners, adding to the Tower of London's reputation as a place of incarceration.

The walls of the Tower of London enclose the entire complex, forming a defensive perimeter. These walls consist of a combination of stone and earthwork, reinforced with bastions and battlements. Visitors can walk along the wall's upper walkway, offering panoramic views of the surrounding area and providing a sense of the fortress's vastness.

3.3 THE INNER WARD

The Inner Ward of the Tower of London encompasses the central area within the fortified walls. It comprises the White Tower, along with several courtyards, buildings, and structures of historical significance. This section of the complex was primarily used for royal residence, administration, and governance.

Within the Inner Ward, visitors can explore notable structures such as the Medieval Palace, the Jewel House, the Great Hall, and the Royal Mint. The Medieval Palace, as mentioned earlier, served as a residence for royalty and showcases the opulent living quarters of medieval monarchs. The Great Hall, situated adjacent to the White Tower in the Inner Ward, served as a grand assembly space for feasts, ceremonies, and important gatherings. The hall features a large open area with a raised dais at one end where the king or queen would sit.

The Jewel House, another significant structure within the Inner Ward, is where the Crown Jewels of the United Kingdom are displayed. This exhibition showcases a breathtaking collection of precious gems, crowns, scepters, and other regalia used in coronations and royal ceremonies. Visitors can marvel at the dazzling display and learn about the history and symbolism behind these revered objects.

The Inner Ward also includes a range of courtyards and gardens, providing tranquil spaces amidst the imposing architecture. These green areas offer visitors a chance to relax and appreciate the historical ambiance of the Tower of London. One such courtyard is the Wakefield Tower Green, an enclosed garden adjacent to the Wakefield Tower, providing a serene retreat within the fortress.

3.4 THE OUTER WARD:

Beyond the Inner Ward lies the Outer Ward, which covers a larger area and includes various structures, open spaces, and defensive elements.

This section of the Tower of London served more practical and utilitarian purposes, such as storage, workshops, and accommodations for soldiers and officials.

The Outer Ward houses structures like the White Tower Wharf, where supplies and materials were unloaded from the river and transported into the fortress. It also includes the Salt Tower, located at the corner of the outer curtain wall, which served as both a storage facility and a defensive fortification.

Other buildings in the Outer Ward include the Royal Armories, where weapons and armor were stored and maintained, and the Queen's House, a residence for high-ranking officials and the Lieutenant of the Tower. The Queen's House features elegant architecture and serves as a reminder of the Tower of London's royal connections.

The Outer Ward also features a spacious parade ground known as the Tower Green. This open area was used for military drills, parades, and public ceremonies. It is also famous for being the site of various notable executions, including those of Anne Boleyn and Lady Jane Grey, making it a place of historical significance.

3.5 CROWN JEWELS EXHIBITION:

The Crown Jewels Exhibition, located within the Jewel House in the Inner Ward, is a major highlight of the Tower of London. This exhibition showcases a stunning collection of precious jewels, crowns, and ceremonial regalia that are an integral part of the British monarchy.

Visitors to the Crown Jewels Exhibition can witness the splendor and magnificence of the Crown Jewels, which include the Imperial State Crown, the Sovereign's Scepter, the Queen's Crown, and numerous other crowns and tiaras. These intricate and meticulously crafted items are adorned with precious gemstones, such as diamonds, rubies, sapphires, and pearls.

The exhibition provides a glimpse into the history and symbolism associated with the Crown Jewels. Visitors can learn about their use in coronations, royal ceremonies, and the representation of the monarch's authority and sovereignty. The Crown Jewels Exhibition offers a unique opportunity to appreciate the craftsmanship, beauty, and cultural significance of these treasured artifacts.

Overall, the Tower of London's architecture and layout encompass a rich tapestry of historical and architectural elements. From the imposing White Tower to the intricate towers and walls, each structure tells a story of the fortress's evolution over centuries. The Inner Ward and Outer Ward provide a glimpse into the lives of royalty, the administration of power, and the function of the fortress. And within the Jewel House, the Crown Jewels Exhibition stands as a testament to the regal grandeur and enduring heritage of the British monarchy.

4.0 KEY ATTRACTION AND HIGHLIGHTS OF THE TOWER OF LONDON

4.1 THE WHITE TOWER, ROYAL ARMORIES AND MUSEUM

The White Tower, the iconic centerpiece of the Tower of London, is a must-visit attraction for history enthusiasts. Built by William the Conqueror in the late 11th century, this formidable stone fortress offers visitors a glimpse into the past with its impressive Royal Armories and Museum.

The Royal Armories and Museum within the White Tower houses an extensive collection of arms, armor, and other military artifacts dating back centuries. It showcases the evolution of weaponry and provides insight into the military history of England. Visitors can marvel at the magnificent displays of swords, shields, suits of armor, crossbows, and firearms, which offer a fascinating look into the craftsmanship and technology of different eras.

The museum also presents a unique opportunity to explore the lives of medieval kings and warriors. Visitors can learn about famous historical figures, such as King Henry VIII, who is known for his extravagant armor on display. The White Tower provides a captivating experience for anyone interested in the military history of England.

4.2 CROWN JEWELS: THE JEWEL HOUSE

The Tower of London is home to the Crown Jewels of the United Kingdom, which are displayed in the Jewel House. The Crown Jewels represent the regalia used in the coronation of British monarchs and include dazzling crowns, scepters, orbs, swords, and other ceremonial objects.

Visitors can witness the breathtaking beauty of these priceless treasures, which include the Imperial State Crown, worn by the current monarch during the State Opening of Parliament. The Crown Jewels are adorned with an array of precious gemstones, including diamonds, rubies, sapphires, and emeralds. The opulence and craftsmanship of these jewels are truly awe-inspiring.

The Jewel House provides a fascinating insight into the monarchy and the traditions that surround it. Visitors can learn about the history behind the Crown Jewels and the significance of each piece. The security measures and the tales of attempted theft add an extra layer of intrigue to the experience.

4.3 TOWER GREEN: EXECUTION SITE

Tower Green, a tranquil garden area within the Tower of London, holds a dark and chilling history as the site of numerous executions. This spot has witnessed the end of several high-profile figures throughout history.

One of the most famous executions that took place at Tower Green was that of Anne Boleyn, the second wife of King Henry VIII. Her beheading in 1536 is just one of the many stories of intrigue, betrayal, and power struggles associated with this haunting location.

Visitors to Tower Green can stand on the very ground where these historical events unfolded. The solemn atmosphere and the memorials erected in honor of the executed individuals create a poignant reminder of the Tower's past. Exploring this site offers a chance to reflect on the darker aspects of England's history.

4.4 MEDIEVAL PALACE: THE WAKEFIELD TOWER AND ST THOMAS TOWER

The Tower of London is not just a fortress; it also houses remnants of medieval royal residences. The Wakefield Tower and St. Thomas's Tower, located within the complex, provide a glimpse into the opulent lifestyle of the kings and queens of the past.

The Wakefield Tower, named after the Duke of Clarence, was originally built as a luxurious residence for royalty. It features beautiful vaulted ceilings, fireplaces, and a magnificent chapel. Visitors can explore the tower and imagine the lavish surroundings that once hosted kings and queens.

St. Thomas's Tower, also known as the Traitor's Gate, was initially a water entrance to the Tower of London. It later served as a prison for high-profile prisoners. The tower's dark and ominous ambiance serves as a stark contrast to the grandeur of the Wakefield Tower.

Exploring these medieval palaces allows visitors to immerse themselves in the rich history and grandeur of the Tower of London. The intricate architectural details, such as the carved stone work and the ornate decorations, transport visitors back in time to an era of regal splendor.

As visitors wander through the Wakefield Tower, they can envision the extravagant feasts and gatherings that took place within its walls. The grandeur of the chapel, with its beautiful stained glass windows and intricate woodwork, provides a sense of the religious significance and the spiritual life of the medieval royals.

On the other hand, St. Thomas's Tower offers a different perspective, with its somber atmosphere and associations with imprisonment and treason. The Traitor's Gate, through which many prisoners entered the tower, is a poignant reminder of the Tower's darker history. Exploring the tower's narrow chambers and narrow windows evokes a sense of confinement and isolation, allowing visitors to imagine the harsh conditions endured by those imprisoned within its walls.

4.5 THE YEOMAN WARDERS (BEEFEATERS)

A visit to the Tower of London wouldn't be complete without encountering the iconic Yeoman Warders, commonly known as

Beefeaters. These ceremonial guards are an integral part of the Tower's history and tradition.

The Yeoman Warders have a fascinating role as both guides and guardians of the Tower. Dressed in their distinctive red and gold uniforms, they provide captivating guided tours, sharing tales of the Tower's past and its notable residents. With their extensive knowledge and charismatic storytelling, the Yeoman Warders bring history to life, entertaining visitors with anecdotes, legends, and historical facts.

These knowledgeable guides offer a unique perspective on the Tower's history, offering insights into the daily life, intrigues, and even ghost stories associated with this historic site. Their presence adds a touch of authenticity and charm, enhancing the overall visitor experience.

4.6 THE RAVENS OF THE TOWER

One of the most intriguing and enduring legends of the Tower of London revolves around its resident ravens. According to the legend, if the ravens were to ever leave the Tower, the kingdom would fall.

The Tower is home to a group of captive ravens, with their wings clipped to prevent them from flying away. These mystical birds, known as the "Guardians of the Tower," are cared for by the Ravenmaster, a position that has been held for centuries. The Ravenmaster ensures their well-being and upholds the tradition associated with these enigmatic creatures.

Visitors to the Tower can witness the ravens firsthand as they roam freely within their designated area. The sight of these majestic birds, with their glossy black feathers and piercing gaze, creates an air of mystique and intrigue. The Ravenmaster himself often provides fascinating insights into the history and folklore surrounding the ravens, adding to their allure.

The ravens have become a beloved symbol of the Tower of London, capturing the imagination of visitors and adding an element of mystery to the overall experience. Their presence is a reminder of the deep-rooted traditions and legends that continue to resonate within the walls of this historic fortress.

In conclusion, the Tower of London offers a wealth of attractions and highlights that cater to a wide range of interests. From the historical significance of the White Tower and its Royal Armories to the dazzling Crown Jewels displayed in the Jewel House, visitors can immerse themselves in centuries of British history and royalty. The Tower Green serves as a solemn reminder of the tower's darker past, while the medieval palaces of Wakefield Tower and St. Thomas's Tower provide a glimpse into the opulence and grandeur of the medieval monarchy. The presence of the Yeoman Warders and the legend of the Ravens of the Tower add a touch of authenticity and mystique, making a visit to the Tower of London an unforgettable experience.

5.0 GUIDED TOURS AND VISITOR EXPERIENCE

5.1 OPENING HOURS AND ADMISSION

The Tower of London, one of the most iconic landmarks in the city, has a rich history dating back nearly a millennium. As a popular tourist attraction and historic site, it attracts millions of visitors each year who are eager to explore its fascinating past and marvel at its architectural splendor. If you're planning a visit to the Tower of London, it's essential to know about its opening hours and admission details to make the most of your experience.

OPENING HOURS:
The Tower of London typically opens its doors to visitors from Tuesday to Saturday, with adjusted hours on Sundays and Mondays. However, it's important to note that opening hours can vary depending on the season, special events, and any unforeseen circumstances. Therefore, it is always recommended to check the official Tower of London website or contact their visitor information line for the most up-to-date information before your visit.

On most days, the Tower opens at 9:00 a.m., providing an early start to your exploration. Closing times also vary depending on the time of year, with the Tower typically closing between 4:30 p.m. and 5:30 p.m. Again, these times are subject to change, so it's crucial to confirm the precise opening and closing hours before your visit.

ADMISSION AND TICKETING:

To gain entry into the Tower of London, visitors are required to purchase tickets. There are several options available for ticket purchase, including online bookings, on-site ticket offices, and authorized resellers. Booking your tickets in advance, especially during peak tourist seasons or holidays, is highly recommended to avoid long queues and ensure availability.

The Tower of London offers different ticket types to accommodate various preferences and interests. These ticket options may include:

Standard Admission: This ticket grants access to the main highlights of the Tower, such as the White Tower, Crown Jewels exhibition, medieval palace, and the famous ravens. It allows visitors to explore the Tower at their own pace.

Guided Tour: For those seeking a more immersive experience, guided tours are available. Led by Yeoman Warders, often referred to as "Beefeaters," these tours provide in-depth knowledge about the Tower's history, traditions, and intriguing stories. Guided tours are typically included in the price of admission.

Special Exhibitions: The Tower of London occasionally hosts temporary exhibitions that delve into specific aspects of its history or showcase unique artifacts. These exhibitions may require a separate ticket or an additional fee on top of the standard admission.

Family Tickets: Families visiting the Tower of London can benefit from discounted family tickets, allowing both adults and children to enjoy the experience together.

It's important to note that prices for tickets can vary depending on factors such as age, residency status, and any additional services or experiences included. For the most accurate and up-to-date information on ticket prices, it is advisable to visit the official Tower of London website or contact their visitor information line.

Once inside the Tower of London, visitors are free to explore its various attractions, including the iconic White Tower, the medieval walls, the historic armory, and the Crown Jewels exhibition. The Tower also hosts a range of live reenactments, exhibitions, and activities throughout the year, making each visit a unique and immersive experience.

Visiting the Tower of London provides an extraordinary opportunity to step back in time and discover the stories, legends, and secrets of this historic fortress. By familiarizing yourself with the opening hours and admission details, you can plan your visit effectively, maximize your time, and ensure a memorable experience exploring one of London's most treasured landmarks.

5.2 BEEFEATER-LED TOURS

Beefeater-led tours at the Tower of London offer visitors a captivating and immersive experience in one of the most iconic historical landmarks in the world. These tours, led by the Yeoman Warders, known as Beefeaters, provide a unique opportunity to delve into the rich history, legends, and tales surrounding the Tower.

The Tower of London, located on the north bank of the River Thames in central London, has a history spanning over 900 years. Originally built as a royal palace, it has served various purposes throughout its existence, including a royal mint, treasury, prison, and even a menagerie. Today, it is primarily known as a historic site and home to the Crown Jewels of the United Kingdom.

The Beefeaters, with their distinctive red and gold uniforms, are an integral part of the Tower's identity. They have been a part of the Tower's history for centuries and are responsible for guarding the Crown Jewels and the security of the Tower. In addition to their ceremonial duties, Beefeaters also serve as tour guides, sharing their vast knowledge and passion for the Tower's history with visitors.

A Beefeater-led tour typically begins at the main entrance of the Tower, where visitors are greeted by their guide. The tours usually last around an hour and cover key areas of the Tower, including the White Tower, the Medieval Palace, the Bloody Tower, and the Chapel of St. Peter ad Vincula. These areas are steeped in history and hold stories of royal intrigue, imprisonment, and execution.

As visitors walk through the Tower, the Beefeater guide brings the past to life with vivid storytelling and anecdotes. They provide fascinating insights into the lives of the Tower's former inhabitants, such as famous prisoners like Anne Boleyn, Sir Walter Raleigh, and Guy Fawkes. The Beefeaters' deep knowledge of the

Tower's history allows them to share lesser-known stories and legends that captivate the imagination.

The tour also includes a visit to the Crown Jewels, which are housed in the Jewel House. The Beefeater guide shares the history and significance of these dazzling treasures, including the Crown, Scepter, and Orb, which are used during the coronation of British monarchs. Visitors can marvel at the exquisite craftsmanship and learn about the elaborate security measures in place to protect these priceless artifacts.

One of the highlights of the Beefeater-led tours is witnessing the Ceremony of the Keys, an ancient tradition that has taken place every night for over 700 years. The ceremony involves the formal locking of the Tower gates, and a small group of visitors is selected to witness this exclusive event, led by a Yeoman Warder. The Beefeater guide provides historical context and sets the scene for this unique experience.

Throughout the tour, visitors have the opportunity to ask questions and interact with the Beefeater guide. Their enthusiasm, humor, and deep knowledge create an engaging and enjoyable atmosphere. Visitors leave with a greater understanding of the Tower's history, its role in shaping British history, and a renewed appreciation for this iconic landmark.

It's worth noting that while the Beefeater-led tours are informative and entertaining, they can be popular and busy, especially during peak tourist seasons. It's advisable to book tickets in advance or arrive early to secure a spot on the tour. Additionally, photography restrictions may apply in certain areas of the Tower, such as the Jewel House, for security and conservation reasons.

In conclusion, Beefeater-led tours at the Tower of London offer an immersive and educational experience that takes visitors on a journey through centuries of history. The expertise, storytelling prowess, and passion of the Beefeaters make these tours a must-do for anyone interested in British history, royal traditions, and the captivating tales of the Tower.

5.3 AUDIO GUIDES AND MULTIMEDIA EXHIBIT

The Tower of London, with its rich history spanning over a thousand years, is an iconic landmark and one of the most visited tourist attractions in London. To enhance visitors' experience and provide them with a deeper understanding of the tower's history and significance, the Tower of London offers audio guides and multimedia exhibits. These immersive tools allow visitors to engage with the exhibits in a more interactive and informative manner, making their visit truly unforgettable.

The audio guide is a popular feature that provides visitors with a narrated tour of the Tower of London. Upon arrival, visitors are typically given a portable audio device with a set of headphones. The audio guide offers a range of languages to accommodate the diverse array of visitors from around the world. This ensures that everyone can fully immerse themselves in the history and stories of the tower, regardless of their native language.

The audio guide at the Tower of London takes visitors on a journey through its many significant sites and buildings. It provides a wealth of historical information, fascinating anecdotes, and captivating stories associated with each location. As visitors explore the tower, they can listen to the audio guide at their own pace, pausing or rewinding as they wish. This flexibility allows visitors to delve deeper into areas of personal interest or spend more time absorbing the atmosphere of particular spots.

The audio guide highlights key attractions within the Tower of London, such as the White Tower, the Crown Jewels, the Bloody Tower, and the Chapel of St. Peter ad Vincula. It provides historical context, describing the purpose and significance of each site. Visitors can learn about the tower's use as a royal palace, a prison, and a treasury, among other roles it has played throughout history. The audio guide brings to life the stories of the people who lived and died within its walls, including monarchs, prisoners, and guards, adding a sense of human connection to the historical facts.

In addition to the audio guide, the Tower of London also incorporates multimedia exhibits to create a more interactive and immersive experience. These exhibits utilize state-of-the-art technology to engage visitors in a dynamic and educational way. The multimedia elements include interactive displays, touchscreens, videos, and animations that complement the historical artifacts and information.

One notable multimedia exhibit at the Tower of London is the virtual reconstruction of significant events. Through the use of advanced visual effects and computer-generated imagery, visitors can witness historical moments as if they were happening right in front of them. For example, visitors may be able to witness the coronation of a monarch, experience the Great Fire of London, or even observe a medieval jousting tournament. These virtual reconstructions provide a vivid and memorable experience that transports visitors back in time and enables them to better understand the historical context of the tower.

Furthermore, the multimedia exhibits also include in-depth presentations about the tower's architecture, construction techniques, and restoration efforts. Visitors can explore interactive models and displays that demonstrate the evolution of the tower over the centuries. These exhibits shed light on the engineering marvels and the intricate details of the tower's design, enabling visitors to appreciate the craftsmanship and ingenuity that went into its construction.

The Tower of London's audio guide and multimedia exhibits ensure that visitors have a comprehensive and engaging experience during their visit. By combining historical narratives, interactive displays, and virtual reconstructions, these tools provide a multi-sensory approach to learning about the tower's past. They cater to different learning styles and interests, making the attraction accessible and enjoyable for people of all ages and backgrounds.

Overall, the audio guide and multimedia exhibits at the Tower of London greatly enrich the visitor experience. They bring history to life, offering a captivating and educational journey through the tower's storied past. Whether it's listening to the tales of long-gone monarchs or witnessing virtual recreations of significant events, these tools create an immersive and engaging atmosphere that allows visitors to connect with the Tower of London on a deeper level.

One of the advantages of the audio guide and multimedia exhibits is their ability to provide a personalized experience. Each visitor can choose their own path through the tower, selecting the areas and topics that interest them the most. The audio guide offers a flexible and self-paced tour, allowing visitors to spend more time exploring areas that intrigue them and skipping over sections that may be less relevant to their interests. This customization ensures that every visitor can have a tailored experience that aligns with their preferences and curiosity.

Moreover, the audio guide and multimedia exhibits serve as valuable educational tools. They go beyond simple facts and dates, offering in-depth explanations and analysis of the historical context surrounding the Tower of London. Visitors can gain insights into the political, social, and cultural dynamics of different time periods, understanding how the tower played a role in shaping the history of England. By combining audio narration, visual aids, and interactive elements, these tools facilitate a more profound comprehension of the tower's significance and its place in British history.

The audio guide also enhances the overall visitor experience by providing a sense of immersion and storytelling. The narrators, often historians or actors, lend their voices to the audio guide, infusing the stories with passion and emotion. Their engaging delivery captivates visitors, transporting them back in time and creating a connection between the past and the present. Visitors can almost envision the events and people described, fostering a more profound appreciation for the tower's historical heritage.

Furthermore, the multimedia exhibits offer a multi-sensory experience that stimulates different aspects of learning. Visitors can interact with touchscreens, allowing them to delve deeper into specific topics, view images, and access additional information. Videos and animations provide dynamic visuals that bring historical events and architectural details to life. These visual and tactile elements cater to a variety of learning styles, making the information more accessible and engaging for a wide range of visitors.

The Tower of London's audio guide and multimedia exhibits also serve as valuable preservation tools. By incorporating digital technologies, the tower can present historical information and artifacts in a manner that is both engaging and sustainable. Fragile or sensitive artifacts can be protected from excessive handling and exposure by offering digital replicas or detailed visual representations. Additionally, the audio guide and multimedia exhibits can be regularly updated or expanded to incorporate new research and discoveries, ensuring that visitors receive the most accurate and up-to-date information.

In conclusion, the audio guide and multimedia exhibits at the Tower of London enhance the visitor experience by providing a rich and immersive exploration of its history and significance. Through personalized audio tours, virtual reconstructions, interactive displays, and engaging storytelling, visitors can gain a deeper understanding of the tower's past and the people who shaped its destiny. These tools create a dynamic and educational atmosphere, allowing visitors of all ages and backgrounds to connect with the tower's historical heritage in a meaningful way. The audio guide and multimedia exhibits not only enrich the visitor experience but also contribute to the preservation and dissemination of the tower's rich cultural legacy.

5.4 TOWER BRIDGE EXHIBITION

The Tower of London Bridge, also known simply as the Tower Bridge, is one of the most iconic landmarks in London, England. It is a combined bascule and suspension bridge that spans the River Thames, connecting the City of London with the borough of Southwark. While the Tower Bridge itself is a marvel of engineering and architecture, it is also home to a fascinating exhibition that offers visitors a glimpse into the bridge's history, construction, and operation.

The Tower Bridge Exhibition is located within the two towers of the bridge, providing visitors with an immersive and educational experience. The exhibition explores the bridge's origins, the challenges faced during its construction, and its importance as a vital transportation link in the heart of London.

One of the highlights of the exhibition is the historical section, which delves into the fascinating story behind the creation of the Tower Bridge. Visitors can learn about the 19th-century dilemma of increasing commercial activity on the Thames, which necessitated the construction of a new bridge. The exhibition showcases the original architectural drawings, photographs, and documents that shed light on the bridge's design process and the people involved in its construction.

Visitors can also explore the engineering marvels of the Tower Bridge through interactive displays and models. These exhibits explain the innovative mechanisms behind the bridge's operation, including the hydraulic system that powers the raising and lowering of the bascules, or the moving sections of the bridge. The exhibition provides a behind-the-scenes look at the engineering ingenuity that went into creating this iconic structure.

For those interested in the bridge's operation, the exhibition offers a rare opportunity to see the inner workings of the Tower Bridge. Visitors can access the high-level walkways, situated 42 meters above the river, which offer breathtaking panoramic views of London. They can witness the bascules being raised and lowered, experience the vibration of the engines, and even observe the bridge from the glass floor sections, providing a unique perspective of the bustling river below.

The Tower Bridge Exhibition also showcases the rich history and cultural significance of the bridge. Visitors can explore the Victorian Engine Rooms, which house the original steam engines that powered the bridge until 1976. These rooms are a testament to the bridge's historical heritage and the transition from steam power to modern technology.

The exhibition incorporates multimedia presentations, films, and interactive displays that bring the bridge's history and significance to life. Visitors can listen to personal accounts of former bridge workers, discover stories of notable events that took place at the bridge, and learn about the bridge's symbolic importance as a symbol of London.

The permanent exhibition, the Tower Bridge also hosts temporary displays and special events throughout the year. These exhibits often focus on different aspects of the bridge's history, architecture, or the cultural heritage of London. From art exhibitions to historical retrospectives, there is always something new to discover at the Tower Bridge.

The Tower Bridge Exhibition offers a captivating journey into the past, present, and future of one of London's most iconic landmarks. It combines historical artifacts, interactive displays, and stunning views to provide visitors with a comprehensive understanding of the bridge's construction, operation, and cultural significance. Whether you are a history enthusiast, an engineering buff, or simply a curious traveler, the Tower Bridge Exhibition is a must-visit destination that showcases the grandeur and beauty of this iconic structure.

5.5 SPECIAL EVENTS AND REENACTMENTS

Throughout the year, the Tower of London hosts a variety of special events and reenactments that offer a unique and immersive experience for visitors. These events range from historical reenactments of significant moments in the Tower's past to live performances, exhibitions, and themed activities.

For example, during certain times of the year, visitors may have the opportunity to witness the Ceremony of the Keys, a centuries-old tradition where the Tower is locked up for the night. This ceremonial event involves the Chief Yeoman Warder leading a group of Yeoman Warders in a procession to secure the Tower's gates, accompanied by military precision and historic rituals. The Ceremony of the Keys is a highly sought-after event, and advanced booking is required to attend.

Other special events at the Tower of London may include historical reenactments showcasing pivotal moments from the Tower's past, such as the execution of famous prisoners or battles that took place within its walls. These reenactments provide a vivid and engaging way to learn about the Tower's history and bring its stories to life.

Additionally, the Tower hosts temporary exhibitions that explore specific themes or historical periods. These exhibitions often feature artifacts, interactive displays, and multimedia presentations to provide a deeper understanding of the Tower's significance and the events that unfolded there.

Visitors are advised to check the Tower of London's official website or inquire about upcoming events and exhibitions to plan their visit accordingly and ensure they don't miss out on these unique experiences.

The Tower of London offers a range of guided tours, audio guides, multimedia exhibits, and special events to enhance the visitor experience. Whether exploring the Tower with a knowledgeable Beefeater, immersing oneself in the interactive displays, or witnessing historical reenactments, visitors can delve into the rich history of this iconic landmark. The Tower of London truly provides an unforgettable journey through time, allowing visitors to connect with centuries of British history and experience the grandeur and intrigue of one of London's most treasured sites.

6.0 PRACTICAL INFORMATION FOR VISITORS

6.1 GETTING TO THE TOWER OF LONDON:

As a UNESCO World Heritage Site and a popular tourist attraction, transportation to the Tower of London is readily available and can be accessed through various means. Let's explore the different transportation options for reaching the Tower of London.

Underground/Metro:

The London Underground, also known as the Tube, is one of the most convenient and efficient ways to travel within the city. The Tower Hill tube station, served by the District and Circle lines, is the closest station to the Tower of London. From there, it's just a short walk across Tower Hill to reach the entrance of the Tower.

Bus:

London's extensive bus network covers almost every corner of the city, including the Tower of London. Several bus routes pass near the Tower, with stops at Tower Hill or nearby locations. Bus services provide a scenic way to reach the Tower, allowing you to enjoy the cityscape along the way.

River Thames Boats:

Since the Tower of London is situated on the banks of the River Thames, riverboats offer a unique and picturesque mode of transportation. Various boat operators offer regular services along the river, including stops near the Tower. These boats often provide both commuter and tourist services, allowing visitors to enjoy a leisurely journey while taking in the iconic London landmarks.

Taxi or Rideshare:

Taxis are a convenient option for reaching the Tower of London, especially if you have heavy luggage or prefer a door-to-door service. London's iconic black cabs are widely available, and rideshare services like Uber are also popular in the city. Simply input the

Tower of London as your destination, and the driver will take you directly to the entrance.

Walking and Cycling:

If you're in the vicinity of central London, walking or cycling to the Tower of London can be an enjoyable and eco-friendly option. The Tower is well-connected by pedestrian-friendly paths and cycle lanes. Several docking stations for bike-sharing schemes, such as Santander Cycles, can be found nearby, allowing you to rent a bike for a short period.

Car:

While the Tower of London is accessible by car, it's important to note that the area can have heavy traffic, limited parking spaces, and congestion charges. However, if you choose to drive, there are parking facilities available nearby. It's advisable to check parking availability and fees in advance.

Guided Tours:

Many tour operators offer comprehensive sightseeing tours of London, including visits to the Tower of London. These tours often provide transportation to and from the Tower, along with a knowledgeable guide who shares fascinating historical insights and stories about the landmark.

It's worth noting that the Tower of London is located in a busy area of the city, and during peak tourist seasons, the surrounding roads and attractions can be crowded. It's advisable to plan your visit in advance, considering factors such as transportation availability, timing, and any events or road closures that might affect your journey.

Overall, the Tower of London is easily accessible via a range of transportation options, catering to various preferences and needs. Whether you choose to travel by underground, bus, boat, taxi, or even on foot or bicycle, you'll have no trouble reaching this iconic historical site and immersing yourself in its rich heritage.

6.2 TICKETS AND ADMISSION PRICES:

The Tower of London, located in the heart of London, England, is an iconic historic site that attracts millions of visitors each year. It is a UNESCO World Heritage site and one of the city's most popular tourist destinations. When planning a visit to the Tower of London, it's essential to have information about ticket and admission prices to make the most of your experience.

Ticket and admission prices for the Tower of London can vary based on several factors, including age, residency, and the type of ticket you choose. The following information provides an overview of the pricing structure as of my knowledge cutoff in September 2021, but please note that prices may have changed since then. It is always a good idea to check the official website for the most up-to-date information.

STANDARD ADMISSION:
The standard admission ticket grants access to all the main attractions and exhibits within the Tower of London. The prices for standard admission are typically as follows:
Adult (age 18-64): £25 (approximately $35)
Child (age 5-15): £12.50 (approximately $17)
Senior (age 65+): £20.50 (approximately $28)
Student (with valid ID): £20.50 (approximately $28)

FAMILY TICKETS:
Family tickets offer discounted rates for families visiting the Tower of London together. The family ticket prices are usually as follows:
Family of 1 adult and up to 3 children: £37.50 (approximately $52)
Family of 2 adults and up to 3 children: £64.00 (approximately $89)

MEMBERSHIP AND ANNUAL PASSES:
For those planning multiple visits or interested in exploring the Tower of London in-depth, membership and annual passes can offer excellent value. The prices for membership and annual passes may vary based on the level of access and additional benefits provided.

ONLINE DISCOUNTS AND SPECIAL OFFERS:
It is worth checking the official website of the Tower of London for any online discounts or special offers available during your visit. Sometimes, advanced online bookings can

provide discounted prices or exclusive packages, allowing you to save money and enhance your experience.

ADDITIONAL EXPERIENCES:
While the standard admission ticket covers most of the Tower's attractions, certain experiences within the Tower may require separate tickets or additional fees. For example, access to the famous Crown Jewels exhibition may be included in the standard admission, but special events, tours, or exhibitions might have separate charges.

Please note that the Tower of London's ticket and admission prices are subject to change, and it is always advisable to verify the latest information before planning your visit. The official website of the Tower of London (www.hrp.org.uk/tower-of-london) provides comprehensive details about ticket prices, opening hours, and any additional information you may require.

Visiting the Tower of London is an incredible opportunity to explore centuries of history, see the iconic Crown Jewels, and immerse yourself in the stories of kings, queens, and famous prisoners. By understanding the ticket and admission prices, you can plan your visit accordingly and make the most of your time at this remarkable historical landmark.

6.3 VISITOR FACILITIES:

The Tower of London offers a range of facilities to ensure a comfortable visit:

RESTROOMS:

There are restroom facilities available throughout the Tower complex, including accessible toilets and baby-changing facilities.

DINING: The Tower has several dining options, including cafes and a restaurant. You can enjoy a quick snack or a full meal while taking a break from exploring.

SOUVENIR SHOPS: There are gift shops located within the Tower where you can purchase souvenirs, books, and other items related to the Tower's history.

INFORMATION POINTS: Throughout the complex, you'll find information points staffed by knowledgeable personnel who can provide assistance, answer questions, and offer guidance.

AUDIO GUIDES: For a more immersive experience, audio guides are available for rent. These guides provide detailed commentary and insights into the various areas of the Tower.

WI-FI: Free Wi-Fi is available within the Tower complex, allowing visitors to stay connected and share their experiences.

6.4 ACCESSIBILITY INFORMATION:

The Tower of London strives to make the site as accessible as possible for all visitors. Some of the accessibility features and services include:

Wheelchair Accessibility: The majority of the Tower complex is accessible for wheelchair users. However, due to the historic nature of the buildings, some areas may have limited access.

Mobility Aid Rental: Wheelchairs and mobility scooters can be borrowed free of charge from the Welcome Centre. It is recommended to book in advance to ensure availability.

Accessible Toilets: Accessible toilets are available throughout the Tower complex.

Assistance Dogs: Guide dogs and assistance dogs are permitted within the Tower. Water bowls are provided at various locations for their convenience.

Visual and Hearing Impairments: The Tower of London offers resources such as large-print guides and hearing loops to enhance the experience for visitors with visual or hearing impairments.

Sensory Map: A sensory map is available for visitors with autism or sensory processing disorders, highlighting areas that may be particularly stimulating or overwhelming. This map can help visitors plan their visit and navigate the Tower with greater ease.

Seating Areas: There are seating areas available throughout the Tower complex, allowing visitors to take breaks and rest during their visit.

Accessible Routes: The Tower has designated accessible routes that are designed to accommodate visitors with mobility challenges. These routes are indicated by signage and provide smoother pathways with fewer steps or obstacles.

Signage and Information: The Tower of London has clear signage and information boards throughout the site, providing directions and important information in both written and visual formats.

Sensory Break Spaces: For visitors who may need a quiet and calming space, the Tower offers designated sensory break spaces where they can relax and recharge.

It's worth noting that while the Tower of London strives to be accessible to all visitors, the historic nature of the site may present some limitations. Certain areas, such as the medieval towers, may have restricted access or uneven terrain. However, the staff is always ready to assist and provide alternative arrangements whenever possible.

6.5 PHOTOGRAPHY AND FILMING POLICIES:

Photography for personal use is allowed throughout most areas of the Tower of London. However, there are a few restrictions and guidelines to keep in mind:

Photography is not permitted inside the Crown Jewels exhibition. This is to ensure the security and preservation of these precious artifacts.

Flash photography is prohibited in some areas, particularly where it may disturb or damage sensitive materials or artwork.

Tripods and professional filming equipment are generally not allowed without prior permission. If you are planning professional photography or filming, it is recommended to contact the Tower of London in advance to make the necessary arrangements.

Drone photography or filming is strictly prohibited within the Tower complex.

When taking photographs, be considerate of other visitors and avoid blocking pathways or causing inconvenience.

It's important to note that these policies may be subject to change, so it's always a good idea to check with the Tower of London's official website or inquire with the staff for the most up-to-date information regarding photography and filming policies.

By providing these practical information points, visitors to the Tower of London can have a smoother and more enjoyable experience. Whether it's understanding the various transportation options, knowing the ticket prices and facilities available, or being aware of accessibility features and photography policies, visitors can make the most of their time at this iconic historical site.

7.0 NEARBY ATTRACTIONS AND POINT OF INTEREST

7.1. TOWER BRIDGE

Tower Bridge is an iconic symbol of London and is located near the Tower of London, making it a must-visit attraction for travelers in the area. This magnificent bridge crosses the River Thames and offers stunning views of the cityscape. It is a combined bascule and suspension bridge, designed in the Victorian Gothic style.

Visitors to Tower Bridge can explore its walkways, which are elevated above the traffic, providing an excellent vantage point for panoramic views of London's skyline. The high-level walkway offers a glass floor section, allowing visitors to look down and observe the bridge's mechanisms in action.

Inside the bridge, the Tower Bridge Exhibition provides an insight into the history and engineering behind this iconic structure. The exhibition includes interactive displays, videos, and photographs that showcase the bridge's construction, its role in London's transportation network, and memorable moments in its history.

For an unforgettable experience, visitors can also book a tour to access the bridge's bascule chambers, where they can witness the massive machinery that powers the bridge's opening and closing. Additionally, the bridge often hosts special events, such as exhibitions, concerts, and even weddings.

7.2. HMS BELTFAST

Located on the River Thames near the Tower Bridge, HMS Belfast is a floating naval museum that offers a unique opportunity to explore a historic warship. This Royal Navy cruiser played a significant role in World War II, the Korean War, and the Cold War.

Visitors can explore the various decks of the ship, including the captain's cabin, the gun turrets, and the engine rooms. The interactive exhibits on board provide insights into life at sea and the ship's involvement in key naval battles. The museum offers audio guides, allowing visitors to delve into the ship's history at their own pace.

HMS Belfast provides a captivating glimpse into naval warfare and offers panoramic views of the London skyline from its upper decks. The ship's location on the River Thames, adjacent to the Tower of London, makes it a convenient attraction to visit alongside other landmarks in the area.

7.3 ST. KATHARINE DOCKS:

St. Katharine Docks is a picturesque marina located near the Tower of London. It offers a tranquil oasis amidst the bustling city, with its charming waterside setting and vibrant atmosphere. The docks have a rich history dating back to the early 19th century, and today they are a hub for yachts, boats, and waterside activities.

Visitors to St. Katharine Docks can take leisurely strolls along the quayside, admiring the luxurious yachts and historic barges that line the marina. The area is also home to an array of restaurants, cafes, and bars, offering a diverse range of dining options. From traditional British pubs to international cuisine, there is something to suit every palate.

The docks host regular events, including food markets, art exhibitions, and live performances, providing a vibrant atmosphere for visitors to enjoy. It's a great place to relax, unwind, and take in the beautiful surroundings.

7.4 THE SHARD:

Standing at a height of 310 meters (1,017 feet), The Shard is an architectural marvel and the tallest building in the United Kingdom. Located just across the River Thames from the Tower of London, it offers breathtaking views of the city.

Visitors to The Shard can ascend to the viewing platform on the 72nd floor, known as The View from The Shard. From this vantage point, you can enjoy panoramic vistas of London's skyline, including iconic landmarks such as the Tower Bridge, St. Paul's Cathedral, and the Houses of Parliament. On a clear day, the visibility stretches for up to 40 miles, providing an awe-inspiring experience.

The Shard also houses a variety of restaurants and bars, allowing visitors to indulge in fine dining or enjoy a drink with stunning views. From sophisticated restaurants offering exquisite cuisine to stylish bars serving craft cocktails, The Shard provides a range of options for a memorable dining experience.

For those seeking a unique adrenaline rush, The Shard offers the opportunity to take part in a thrilling "Shard Climb" experience. Led by experienced guides, participants can scale the external framework of the building and enjoy breathtaking views from an open-air platform located 244 meters (800 feet) above the ground.

7.5 SKY GARDEN:

Situated in the heart of the City of London, just a short distance from the Tower of London, Sky Garden is a unique public space housed within a striking glass dome atop the Walkie Talkie building. As one of the highest public gardens in London, it offers a captivating blend of lush greenery, breathtaking views, and exquisite architecture.

Visitors to Sky Garden can explore the beautifully landscaped gardens, featuring an array of tropical plants, flowers, and trees. The garden spans three levels, with observation decks offering panoramic views of London's skyline, including landmarks such as the Tower Bridge, the Gherkin, and the Shard.

The space also encompasses several restaurants, bars, and cafes, where visitors can enjoy a meal, a cup of coffee, or a cocktail while taking in the spectacular surroundings. Whether it's a leisurely brunch, an evening cocktail, or a romantic dinner, Sky Garden provides a range of dining options to suit different tastes and occasions.

In addition to its stunning views and dining offerings, Sky Garden hosts a variety of events, including live music performances, yoga sessions, and art exhibitions. These events add to the vibrant and dynamic atmosphere of this unique attraction.

Exploring the nearby attractions and points of interest around the Tower of London offers visitors a diverse range of experiences. From iconic landmarks like Tower Bridge and The Shard to historical gems like HMS Belfast and the tranquil St. Katharine Docks, there is something to captivate every traveler. And for those seeking breathtaking views and lush green spaces, Sky Garden provides an extraordinary oasis in the heart of the city. These attractions combine history, architecture, and natural beauty to offer an unforgettable visit to this iconic area of London.

8.0 PREPARING FOR YOUR TRIP

8.1 BEST TIME TO VISIT:

The Tower of London is an iconic historical landmark located in the heart of London, England. As one of the city's most popular tourist attractions, it is important to consider the best time to visit in order to make the most of your experience. Several factors come into play when determining the ideal time to explore the Tower of London, including weather conditions, crowds, and special events. Let's delve into each of these aspects to help you plan your visit effectively.

WEATHER CONDITIONS:

London's weather can be quite unpredictable, but generally, the summer months (June to August) offer the most favorable conditions for visiting the Tower of London. During this time, you can expect relatively mild temperatures, with an average high of around 20-25 degrees Celsius (68-77 degrees Fahrenheit). The longer daylight hours also provide ample time to explore the site and its surroundings comfortably. However, it is worth noting that London's summers can sometimes experience periods of rain, so it's advisable to carry an umbrella or raincoat.

CROWDS:

The Tower of London is a popular attraction throughout the year, so it's essential to consider crowd levels when planning your visit. If you prefer a quieter experience with fewer tourists, it is advisable to avoid peak travel seasons, such as summer and school holidays. The site tends to be busiest during weekends and holidays, so visiting on weekdays, particularly during the shoulder seasons of spring (April to May) and autumn (September to October), can help you avoid large crowds.

SPECIAL EVENTS:

The Tower of London hosts various special events and exhibitions throughout the year, which can enhance your visit. These events range from historical reenactments and exhibitions to unique displays of the Crown Jewels. Checking the Tower's official website or contacting their visitor information center in advance will allow you to plan your visit around any special events that may interest you.

TIME OF DAY:

Choosing the right time of day can significantly impact your experience at the Tower of London. Arriving early in the morning, shortly after the site opens, is generally recommended. Doing so allows you to beat the crowds, explore the different sections of the Tower at a leisurely pace, and take advantage of better photo opportunities. Additionally, visiting during the week will help you avoid large tour groups and school field trips.

CHANGING OF THE GUARD:

While the Changing of the Guard ceremony mainly takes place at Buckingham Palace, a similar event known as the Ceremony of the Keys occurs each evening at the Tower of London. This unique ceremony, which has taken place for centuries, involves the locking up of the Tower for the night. Witnessing this traditional event can be a memorable experience and is worth considering when planning your visit. However, it's essential to note that access to the Ceremony of the Keys is limited, and tickets need to be booked well in advance.

In summary, the best time to visit the Tower of London is during the summer months (June to August), preferably on weekdays and early in the morning. This will provide you with comfortable weather conditions, fewer crowds, and ample time to explore the various attractions within the Tower. Additionally, staying updated with the Tower's official website for any special events or exhibitions will allow you to tailor your visit to your interests. Enjoy your time exploring this remarkable historical site!

8.2 PREPARING FOR YOUR VISIT:

Preparing for a trip to the Tower of London can enhance your experience and ensure that you make the most of your visit to this historic landmark. As one of the most iconic attractions in London, the Tower of London offers a glimpse into the city's rich history, with its medieval architecture, royal heritage, and the famous Crown Jewels. Here is an extensive guide to help you prepare for your trip to the Tower of London.

Research and Planning:
Start by conducting thorough research about the Tower of London. Learn about its history, significance, and the various attractions and exhibits it offers. Familiarize yourself with the layout of the complex, including the different towers, courtyards, and museums within the site. Identify the specific areas or exhibits you're

most interested in, so you can prioritize them during your visit.

Booking Tickets:
Check the official Tower of London website or other reliable ticket vendors to purchase your tickets in advance. This step is essential, especially during peak tourist seasons, as it guarantees your entry and helps you avoid long queues. Online tickets often have specific time slots, so plan your visit accordingly.

Choosing the Right Time to Visit:
Consider the time of year and day when planning your trip. The Tower of London can get quite busy, particularly during weekends and holidays. If possible, visit during weekdays or opt for early morning or late afternoon time slots to avoid the crowds. Additionally, check if there are any special events or exhibitions happening during your intended visit, as it may affect the availability and experience.

Transportation and Directions:

Decide on the mode of transportation you'll use to reach the Tower of London. London has an extensive public transportation network, so you can easily reach the site by taking the tube (subway), bus, or even a boat along the River Thames. Use reliable navigation apps or websites to plan your journey and determine the nearest stations or stops to the Tower of London.

Dress Comfortably:

Given the amount of walking you'll do while exploring the Tower of London, it's crucial to wear comfortable clothing and shoes. Opt for weather-appropriate attire and consider the possibility of rain, as the weather in London can be unpredictable. Bring an umbrella or raincoat if needed.

Security and Baggage Restrictions:

The Tower of London has security measures in place, so be prepared to go through a bag check upon entry. To save time, pack light and avoid carrying large backpacks or bags. Note that certain items, such as sharp objects or liquids, may be prohibited. Check the official website for the most up-to-date information on security and baggage restrictions.

Guided Tours and Audio Guides:
Consider taking advantage of guided tours or audio guides available at the Tower of London. These resources provide valuable insights into the history and significance of the site, ensuring you don't miss any important details. Guided tours led by knowledgeable guides can offer a more immersive experience, while audio guides allow you to explore at your own pace.

Food and Refreshments:
While there are several eateries and cafes within the Tower of London complex, it's a good idea to carry a bottle of water and some snacks with you, especially if you plan to spend a significant amount of time exploring the site. This will keep you hydrated and energized throughout your visit.

Photography and Recording:

Capture your memories by bringing a camera or smartphone to take photos and videos. However, be mindful of any photography restrictions in certain areas or exhibits, as the use of flash or tripods may not be allowed. Respect the privacy of others and follow any instructions provided by the staff.

Additional Attractions and Nearby Points of Interest:

The Tower of London is surrounded by other notable landmarks and attractions, such as Tower Bridge, St. Paul's Cathedral, and the Shard. If you have extra time, consider exploring these nearby points of interest to make the most of your visit to the area. Plan your itinerary accordingly to include these additional attractions.

Weather Considerations:

Check the weather forecast for the day of your visit to the Tower of London. London weather can be variable, so it's advisable to dress in layers and carry an umbrella or raincoat if rain is expected. Be prepared for both sunny and rainy conditions to ensure your comfort throughout the day.

Accessibility:
If you or any member of your group has mobility issues or special accessibility requirements, it's essential to plan ahead. The Tower of London offers accessibility features and facilities to accommodate visitors with disabilities. Check the official website or contact the Tower of London directly to inquire about accessibility options, including ramps, elevators, and accessible restrooms.

Children and Family Considerations:
If you're visiting the Tower of London with children, explore family-friendly activities and exhibits offered within the complex. The Tower has interactive displays, engaging storytelling sessions, and even the opportunity to meet costumed characters from history. Consider

checking the website for any special events or activities tailored for younger visitors.

Understanding the History and Significance:
To fully appreciate the Tower of London, take some time to understand its historical significance. Read up on the Tower's role as a royal palace, a prison, and a treasury. Learn about the famous prisoners, such as Anne Boleyn and Sir Walter Raleigh, who were held within its walls. Understanding the context will enrich your experience as you explore the various towers and exhibitions.

Budgeting:
Create a budget for your trip to the Tower of London. In addition to the cost of admission tickets, consider expenses such as transportation, meals, souvenirs, and any additional attractions or events you plan to visit. Having a budget in mind will help you make informed decisions and ensure you have an enjoyable experience without overspending.

Souvenirs and Gift Shops:
The Tower of London has several gift shops where you can purchase souvenirs, books, and replica artifacts. These shops offer a wide range of items related to the Tower's history, British monarchy, and medieval culture. Take some time to browse through these shops and consider picking up a memorable keepsake to commemorate your visit.

Time Allocation:
The Tower of London is a significant historical site with numerous exhibits and attractions. Plan your visit by allocating enough time to explore the various towers, museums, and displays. Consider spending at least a few hours to fully immerse yourself in the rich history and marvel at the Crown Jewels.

Respect the Rules and Etiquette:
While visiting the Tower of London, it's important to respect the rules and etiquette set by the staff. Observe any signage, follow instructions, and be mindful of other visitors.

Remember that the Tower is not only a tourist attraction but also a working royal palace, so be respectful of any restricted areas or ceremonies taking place.

By following these tips and preparing adequately, you can ensure a memorable and fulfilling visit to the Tower of London. Immerse yourself in history, explore the magnificent architecture, and discover the captivating stories behind one of London's most iconic landmarks.

8.3 RECOMMENDED ITINERARY:

The Tower of London is one of the most iconic landmarks in London and a must-visit attraction for history buffs and anyone interested in British heritage. With its rich history spanning nearly a thousand years, this historic fortress has served various purposes throughout the centuries, including a royal palace, a prison, and a treasury. To make the most of your visit to the Tower of London, it's recommended to follow a well-planned itinerary that covers its main highlights and provides a comprehensive understanding of its significance. Here's an extensively detailed recommended itinerary for your visit to the Tower of London:

Arriving at the Tower of London:

- Start your day early to beat the crowds and make the most of your visit.
- The Tower of London is located on the north bank of the River Thames, near the Tower Bridge. The nearest underground station is Tower Hill (District and Circle lines).
- Allow some time to explore the area surrounding the Tower of London, including the picturesque views of the Tower Bridge and the Thames River.

Joining a Guided Tour:

- Consider joining a guided tour led by the Yeoman Warders (also known as Beefeaters). They are informative and entertaining guides who share fascinating stories and insights about the tower's history and its infamous prisoners.
- Guided tours are usually available throughout the day and are included in the price of admission.

Exploring the White Tower:

- The White Tower is the oldest part of the complex and the most iconic structure within the Tower of London. It was built in the 11th century by William the Conqueror.
- Inside the White Tower, you'll find the Royal Armouries collection, which houses an impressive array of arms and armor from different eras.
- Take your time to explore the exhibits and learn about the evolution of weaponry and armor throughout history. Highlights include King Henry VIII's armor and the Line of Kings display.

Discovering the Crown Jewels:

- The Crown Jewels are an essential part of any visit to the Tower of London. They are kept in the Jewel House, located in the Waterloo Block.
- Marvel at the stunning collection of crowns, scepters, orbs, and other royal regalia. The Crown Jewels represent the British monarchy's power and ceremony.
- Be prepared for potential queues, as this is a popular attraction. Consider visiting the Jewel House early in the morning or later in the afternoon to avoid peak times.

Visiting the Medieval Palace:

- Explore the Medieval Palace, situated in the eastern part of the complex, adjacent to the White Tower.
- The palace provides a glimpse into the opulent lifestyle of medieval royalty. Visit the recreated chambers, including the King's Bedchamber, Queen's Presence Chamber, and the Chapel of St. John.

- Admire the medieval architecture, intricate tapestries, and decorative elements that transport you back in time.

Walking the Walls and Towers:

- Take a stroll along the historic walls that surround the Tower of London. The walls provide fantastic views of the city skyline and the surrounding area.
- Explore various towers, such as the Bloody Tower, where the two young princes were imprisoned and presumably murdered, and the famous Traitor's Gate, through which prisoners arrived at the tower by boat.
- Don't miss the iconic Beefeaters guarding the entrances to the towers and learn about their role and traditions.

Exploring the Ravens and Green Spaces:

- The Tower of London is home to a group of famous resident ravens. According to legend, if the ravens ever leave the tower, the kingdom will fall.
- Visit the Raven Enclosure and learn more about these magnificent birds from the Ravenmaster.
- Take a moment to appreciate the beautiful green spaces within the Tower of London grounds. The Tower Green, located in the heart of the complex, is a tranquil area where significant events, including executions, took place. It offers a peaceful retreat from the bustling crowds and an opportunity for reflection.

Exploring the Tower Exhibitions:

- Visit the various exhibitions spread throughout the Tower of London to gain

deeper insights into its history and the lives of its inhabitants.
- The "Coins and Kings: The Royal Mint at the Tower" exhibition showcases the history of currency and the royal minting process.
- The "Medieval Palace: A Palace Fit for a King" exhibition delves into the opulence and daily life of the medieval royal court.
- The "Prisoners of the Tower" exhibition sheds light on the tower's dark history as a place of confinement and torture.

Witnessing the Ceremony of the Keys:

- If you have the opportunity, consider attending the famous Ceremony of the Keys, a centuries-old tradition that takes place every evening before the tower is locked up for the night.
- The ceremony is limited to a small number of ticketed visitors, so it's

essential to book well in advance to secure your spot.

Shopping and Refreshments:

- Before concluding your visit, explore the Tower of London's gift shops, which offer a range of souvenirs, books, and historical memorabilia.
- If you're feeling peckish, there are several cafés and restaurants within the tower's premises where you can grab a snack or enjoy a meal.

Optional: Thames River Cruise:

- Since the Tower of London is situated on the banks of the River Thames, consider taking a leisurely Thames River cruise after your visit.
- Cruise along the river, enjoying panoramic views of London's iconic

landmarks, such as the Houses of Parliament, St. Paul's Cathedral, and the London Eye.
- Remember, the suggested itinerary is extensive, and the amount of time spent at each attraction may vary based on your personal preferences and the pace of your visit. It's advisable to allocate at least half a day to explore the Tower of London thoroughly.

Additionally, always check the official Tower of London website for updated information on opening hours, guided tours, and any temporary exhibitions or events taking place during your visit.

8.4 SAFETY AND SECURITY GUIDELINES:

The Tower of London, located in the heart of London, is an iconic historical landmark that attracts millions of visitors each year. As a site of great historical and cultural significance, ensuring safety and security is of paramount importance. The Tower of London has implemented various guidelines and measures to ensure the safety of visitors, protect the historic artifacts and buildings, and maintain order within the complex. In this article, we will explore the extensive safety and security guidelines at the Tower of London.

ENTRANCE SCREENING:
Upon arrival at the Tower of London, visitors are required to pass through security checkpoints. These checkpoints typically consist of metal detectors and X-ray machines to scan bags and

personal belongings. This screening process helps prevent prohibited items from entering the premises and ensures the safety of all visitors.

PROHIBITED ITEMS:
To maintain safety and security, certain items are strictly prohibited within the Tower of London. These include weapons, sharp objects, flammable substances, explosives, and illegal substances. Visitors are encouraged to review the list of prohibited items before their visit and leave them at home or in their vehicles to avoid any inconvenience.

BAGGAGE RESTRICTIONS:
To streamline the security screening process, visitors are advised to minimize the number of bags and personal belongings they bring to the Tower of London. Large suitcases and oversized backpacks are discouraged as they can impede the flow of foot traffic and cause congestion. It is recommended to carry small bags or backpacks for essentials only.

CCTV SURVEILLANCE

The Tower of London employs an extensive closed-circuit television (CCTV) surveillance system throughout the complex. These cameras are strategically placed to monitor various areas, including entrances, exits, exhibition halls, and public spaces. The CCTV footage is regularly monitored by security personnel to ensure the safety of visitors and the protection of the historical artifacts.

SECURITY PERSONNEL:

Trained security personnel are stationed throughout the Tower of London to provide a visible presence and assist visitors when needed. They are responsible for enforcing security protocols, managing crowd control, and responding to any security incidents or emergencies. Visitors are encouraged to approach security personnel if they have any concerns or require assistance.

EMERGENCY PREPAREDNESS:
The Tower of London maintains robust emergency preparedness measures to handle various situations effectively. Emergency exits and evacuation routes are clearly marked, and visitors are informed about emergency procedures upon entry. In the event of an emergency, such as a fire or an evacuation order, visitors are required to follow the instructions of the security personnel and evacuate the premises calmly and swiftly.

PRESERVATION OF HISTORICAL ARTIFACTS:
In addition to visitor safety, the Tower of London places great emphasis on the preservation and security of its historical artifacts and buildings. Climate control systems are installed to maintain appropriate temperature and humidity levels, ensuring the longevity of delicate items. Display cases, barriers, and alarms are used to protect artifacts from accidental damage or theft.

INFORMATION AND SIGNAGE

Clear and informative signage is placed throughout the Tower of London complex to guide visitors and provide safety-related instructions. Signboards indicate emergency exits, first aid stations, prohibited areas, and other relevant information. Visitors are encouraged to pay attention to these signs and follow the instructions for their own safety and the security of the site.

FIRST AID AND MEDICAL FACILITIES:

The Tower of London has designated first aid stations and medical facilities to provide immediate assistance in case of injuries or medical emergencies. Trained staff members are available to administer first aid and coordinate with emergency services if required. Visitors should notify the nearest staff member or security personnel in the event of an injury or medical issue.

ACCESSIBILITY AND SPECIAL REQUIREMENTS:

The Tower of London strives to provide a safe and enjoyable experience for all visitors, including those with disabilities or special requirements. The complex is equipped with ramps, elevators, and accessible pathways to ensure easy access for wheelchair users and individuals with mobility challenges. Additionally, accessible toilets are available throughout the premises.

FIRE SAFETY:

Fire safety is a critical aspect of the safety guidelines at the Tower of London. The complex is equipped with fire alarms, sprinkler systems, and fire extinguishers to mitigate the risk of fire incidents. Visitors are urged to familiarize themselves with the locations of fire exits and follow the instructions provided in case of a fire emergency.

VISITOR CONDUCT:

Maintaining a safe and secure environment at the Tower of London also depends on the responsible behavior of visitors. All visitors are expected to follow the rules and guidelines set by the management. Running, climbing on structures, touching artifacts, or engaging in disruptive behavior is strictly prohibited. Respecting the historical significance of the site and fellow visitors contributes to a safer and more enjoyable experience for all.

COMMUNICATION AND INFORMATION:

The Tower of London keeps visitors informed about safety and security guidelines through various means of communication. This includes signage, brochures, and announcements. The official website of the Tower of London also provides up-to-date information on safety measures and any specific guidelines or restrictions that may be in place during certain events or exhibitions.

ONGOING TRAINING AND EVALUATION:

The safety and security protocols at the Tower of London are continuously reviewed and updated to adapt to changing circumstances and emerging risks. Security personnel undergo regular training programs to enhance their skills and knowledge in handling security situations. Risk assessments and evaluations are conducted to identify potential vulnerabilities and implement necessary improvements.

COLLABORATION WITH LAW ENFORCEMENT:

The Tower of London maintains a close working relationship with local law enforcement agencies to ensure a coordinated response to any security threats or incidents. This collaboration includes sharing information, conducting joint exercises, and coordinating security measures during high-profile events or visits.

It is essential for visitors to the Tower of London to be aware of and comply with the safety and security guidelines in place. By doing so, visitors can help maintain a secure environment, protect the historical artifacts, and contribute to an enjoyable experience for themselves and others. Remember, the safety and security measures at the Tower of London are in place to ensure the preservation of history and the well-being of all who visit this remarkable landmark. yourself with the location of emergency exits and designated meeting points in case of an emergency. Take note of the nearest First Aid facilities as well.

8.5 SOUVENIRS AND GIFT SHOPS:

The Tower of London, located in the heart of London, England, is a historic fortress and one of the city's most iconic landmarks. Known for its rich history, royal connections, and impressive architecture, the Tower of London attracts millions of visitors each year. Within its walls, visitors can explore various attractions, including the Crown Jewels, medieval towers, and the famous ravens. As with many popular tourist destinations, the Tower of London offers a range of souvenir options and gift shops for visitors to commemorate their visit and take home a piece of history.

Souvenirs and gift shops at the Tower of London provide an opportunity for visitors to find unique and meaningful mementos that reflect the historical and cultural significance of this remarkable place. These shops are strategically located throughout the Tower, making it convenient for visitors to explore and discover the various offerings.

One of the most popular souvenirs at the Tower of London is related to its connection with the British monarchy. Visitors can find a wide range of royal-themed memorabilia, including replicas of the Crown Jewels, miniature figurines of famous British monarchs, and books detailing the history of the royal family. These items allow visitors to capture the grandeur and majesty associated with the Tower's royal heritage.

Another category of souvenirs available at the Tower of London revolves around its historical significance. Visitors can purchase replicas of medieval weapons, armor, and historical artifacts, allowing them to bring home a piece of the Tower's rich past. These items serve as reminders of the Tower's role as a fortress, prison, and palace throughout history.

Additionally, gift shops at the Tower of London offer a wide array of more generic souvenirs, such as t-shirts, magnets, keychains, and postcards. These items often feature iconic images of the Tower of London, including its distinctive towers, the River Thames, or the imposing exterior walls. These souvenirs are popular choices for those seeking simple reminders of their visit or gifts for friends and family back home.

Furthermore, the gift shops at the Tower of London showcase a range of specialty items that cater to specific interests. For example, visitors with a passion for British history might find books on various historical periods, biographies of significant figures, or guides to other historical sites across the United Kingdom. Those interested in the architectural marvels of the Tower can find models or puzzles of the fortress, enabling them to recreate the iconic landmark at home.

The gift shops also prioritize high-quality craftsmanship and locally sourced products. Visitors can find artisanal crafts, such as handmade jewelry, pottery, or textiles, often inspired by the Tower's architecture or historical elements. These items not only make for unique souvenirs but also support local artisans and contribute to the preservation of traditional craftsmanship.

Moreover, the Tower of London's gift shops offer a selection of children's souvenirs, ensuring that younger visitors can find something to commemorate their experience. Toys, games, and educational books centered around the Tower's history and legends are available, allowing children to engage with the site in a fun and interactive way.

It is worth noting that the souvenir and gift shops at the Tower of London can be slightly more expensive compared to similar items found elsewhere in the city. However, the premium cost often reflects the unique nature and historical significance of the products available. The revenue generated from these sales also contributes to the maintenance and conservation of the Tower, ensuring its preservation for future generations.

In conclusion, the souvenir and gift shops at the Tower of London offer a diverse range of items that capture the essence of this iconic landmark. Visitors can find souvenirs related to the monarchy, replicas of historical artifacts, generic mementos, specialty items, and children's souvenirs. Whether seeking a royal-themed keepsake or a tangible connection to the Tower's storied past,

9.0 TOWER OF LONDON IN POP CULTURE

9.1 LITERATURE AND FILM REFERENCES

The Tower of London, a historic castle located in the heart of London, has captured the imagination of writers and filmmakers for centuries. Its rich history, iconic architecture, and dramatic stories of power, betrayal, and intrigue make it a compelling subject for literature and film. Countless references to the Tower of London can be found in various forms of storytelling, including novels, plays, poetry, and movies. In this response, we will explore some notable literature and film references that have immortalized the Tower of London in popular culture.

LITERATURE:

"The Tower of London" by William Harrison Ainsworth: Published in 1840, this historical romance novel tells the story of Lady Jane Grey, a tragic figure in English history who was imprisoned and executed in the Tower. Ainsworth's work popularized the Tower's association with imprisonment and execution, cementing its reputation as a place of horror and despair.

"A Tale of Two Cities" by Charles Dickens: Set during the French Revolution, this classic novel features a significant scene that takes place in the Tower of London. Sydney Carton, one of the main characters, visits Charles Darnay, who is imprisoned in the Tower, in an attempt to save him from the guillotine.

"The Bloody Tower" by Carola Dunn: This historical mystery novel, published in 2003, revolves around a series of murders at the Tower of London during the reign of King Henry VIII. The story weaves together fictional characters and real historical figures to create an atmospheric tale of suspense and intrigue.

"Raven's Gate" by Anthony Horowitz: Part of the "Power of Five" series, this young adult fantasy novel features the Tower of London as a central location. The protagonist, Matt Freeman, becomes embroiled in a battle against dark forces that are trying to unleash evil from within the Tower's walls.

FILM:

"Tower of London" (1939): Directed by Rowland V. Lee, this historical drama film portrays the power struggle between Richard III (played by Basil Rathbone) and his rivals. The Tower of London serves as a backdrop for the dark deeds and political machinations that unfold in the narrative.

"The Private Life of Henry VIII" (1933): Starring Charles Laughton as Henry VIII, this British film features the Tower of London prominently. It depicts the tumultuous life and reign of the infamous king, including his marriages, divorces, and the imprisonment and execution of his wives.

"The Raven" (2012): Directed by James McTeigue, this fictionalized account of Edgar Allan Poe's life intertwines elements of his stories into a murder mystery plot. The climax of the film takes place at the Tower of London, where the protagonist races against time to save a kidnapped woman.

These are just a few examples of the many literature and film references that have showcased the Tower of London. Its imposing architecture, historical significance, and associations with imprisonment and execution have made it an enduring symbol of power and intrigue. Whether in historical novels, thrilling mysteries, or epic dramas, the Tower continues to captivate audiences, bringing its rich history to life on the page and on the screen.

9.2 FAMOUS EVENTS AND LEGENDS:

The Tower of London's long and storied history has given rise to various famous events and legends that continue to capture the public's fascination.

One of the most infamous events associated with the Tower is the imprisonment and execution of royals, nobles, and political figures. Two young princes, Edward V and Richard of Shrewsbury, were famously held in the Tower by their uncle Richard, Duke of Gloucester, who would later become Richard III. The mystery surrounding their disappearance and rumored murder has sparked speculation and inspired many works of fiction.

Another notable event is the execution of Anne Boleyn, the second wife of Henry VIII. Accused of adultery and treason, Anne Boleyn was imprisoned in the Tower before being beheaded in 1536. Her story has been depicted in numerous books, films, and plays, contributing to her enduring legacy.

The legend of the Tower's resident ravens is also a significant part of its folklore. According to the legend, if the ravens were ever to leave the Tower, the kingdom would fall. To ensure their presence, the ravens' wings are clipped to prevent them from flying away. This tradition continues to this day, with a team of dedicated Ravenmasters caring for the ravens.

Furthermore, the Crown Jewels of the United Kingdom are kept within the Tower of London. This collection of precious jewels, including the Imperial State Crown and the Koh-i-Noor diamond, is of immense historical and cultural significance. The ceremony of the Opening of the Tower, where the Crown Jewels are displayed to the public, attracts visitors from all over the world.

9.3 RECENT CULTURAL SIGNIFICANCE:

The Tower of London holds a significant place in history, being one of the most iconic landmarks in London and a UNESCO World Heritage site. Its cultural significance extends beyond its architectural and historical importance. The Tower of London has become a symbol of power, heritage, and the enduring legacy of the British monarchy.

HISTORICAL SIGNIFICANCE:

The Tower of London, founded by William the Conqueror in the 11th century, has witnessed almost a millennium of history. Initially constructed as a fortress, it later served as a royal palace, a treasury, and a prison. Its walls have witnessed the rise and fall of kings and queens, political intrigue, and significant historical events.

The tower's role as a prison is perhaps one of its most well-known aspects. Notorious figures like Anne Boleyn, Lady Jane Grey, and Sir Walter Raleigh were imprisoned within its walls. The tower has also been the site of numerous executions, including those of three queens of England: Anne Boleyn, Catherine Howard, and Lady Jane Grey.

CULTURAL SIGNIFICANCE:

Beyond its historical significance, the Tower of London has a cultural impact that reverberates to this day. It is a living testament to the heritage and traditions of the British monarchy. The crown jewels, housed within the tower, symbolize the regalia of the reigning monarch and are an integral part of royal ceremonies and events.

The Yeoman Warders, commonly known as Beefeaters, who guard the Tower of London, have become iconic figures themselves. Dressed in traditional Tudor-style uniforms, they serve as both guides and custodians of the tower's history. The Yeoman Warders play a vital role in preserving and presenting the tower's cultural significance to visitors from around the world.

The Tower of London's cultural impact is not limited to its historical aspects. It also serves as a popular tourist attraction, drawing millions of visitors annually. Tourists flock to explore the tower's medieval architecture, explore its dark and mysterious history, and witness the Changing of the Guard ceremony.

Additionally, the Tower of London has played a significant role in popular culture. It has featured in numerous books, movies, and television shows, adding to its cultural allure. Its imposing presence, rich history, and association with the British monarchy have made it a symbol of power and intrigue in the collective imagination.

PRESERVATION AND EDUCATIONAL ROLE:

The cultural significance of the Tower of London is further enhanced by its role as a museum and educational institution. The tower's exhibits and displays provide visitors with a unique opportunity to delve into the past and gain a deeper understanding of British history. The White Tower, for example, houses the Royal Armouries collection, displaying a vast array of arms and armor throughout the ages.

Educational programs and guided tours offer insights into the tower's history, architecture, and the lives of the people who inhabited it. These initiatives help preserve and promote cultural awareness, ensuring that the Tower of London remains a living monument to the nation's heritage.

In recent years, efforts have been made to expand the tower's cultural significance by engaging with contemporary issues. Exhibitions exploring themes such as diversity, immigration, and the experiences of different communities have added a dynamic dimension to the Tower of London's cultural offerings. These initiatives reflect a broader societal shift towards inclusivity and the recognition of diverse voices in historical narratives.

In conclusion, the Tower of London holds immense cultural significance as an architectural marvel, a repository of history, and a symbol of the British monarchy. Its historical and cultural impact continues to captivate visitors from all corners of the globe. Through preservation, education, and the exploration of contemporary themes, the Tower of London remains a living testament to the nation's past, present, and future.

10.0 CONCLUSION

10.1 SUMMARY OF KEY POINT

1. Historical Tapestry:

- The Tower of London is a living testament to centuries of British history, with its origins dating back to the Norman Conquest of 1066.

- It has served various roles, including a royal palace, prison, and treasury, making it a multifaceted symbol of power and intrigue.

2. Iconic Architecture:

- The Tower complex comprises multiple towers, with the White Tower standing as the oldest and most iconic.

- The medieval architecture, complete with battlements and turrets, immerses visitors in the atmosphere of a bygone era.

3. Crown Jewels:

- The Tower houses the dazzling Crown Jewels, including the Imperial State Crown and the Sovereign's Sceptre. These symbols of monarchy are on display for visitors to marvel at.

- The exhibit provides insight into the historical and cultural significance of these precious regalia.

4. Yeomen Warders:

- The Yeomen Warders, commonly known as Beefeaters, serve as ceremonial guardians of the Tower. Visitors can engage with them on guided tours, gaining insights into the site's history and folklore.

5. Ravens of the Tower:

- The presence of ravens at the Tower is steeped in legend. According to folklore, if the ravens ever leave, the kingdom will fall. Witnessing these majestic birds adds a touch of mystique to the visit.

6. Interactive Exhibits:

- The Tower offers immersive exhibits that bring history to life, allowing visitors to explore medieval architecture, handle replica armor, and engage in interactive displays.

- The Tower's rich narrative unfolds through multimedia presentations, providing a captivating and educational experience.

7. Panoramic Views:

- Ascend the Tower's battlements for breathtaking panoramic views of the River Thames and the London skyline. The juxtaposition of ancient fortifications against the modern cityscape offers a unique visual experience.

8. Historical Figures and Events:

- The Tower has played a central role in pivotal historical events, including the execution of Anne Boleyn, the imprisonment of Elizabeth I before she became queen, and the mysterious disappearance of the Princes in the Tower.

9. Practical Tips:

- Purchase tickets in advance to avoid long queues.
- Wear comfortable shoes for exploring the extensive grounds.
- Plan for at least half a day to fully absorb the historical richness of the Tower.
- Take advantage of guided tours for a more in-depth understanding of the site.

10. Cultural Significance:
- The Tower of London is a UNESCO World Heritage Site, underscoring its global cultural significance.
- Its role in shaping England's monarchy and the impact of its historical events make it a must-visit destination for cultural enthusiasts.

Embarking on a journey to the Tower of London promises an immersive exploration of England's rich history, offering a captivating blend of architectural splendor, royal heritage, and timeless tales. Visitors are invited to step into the footsteps of kings and queens, unlocking the secrets of a fortress that has stood as witness to centuries of drama and legacy.

In conclusion, the Tower of London stands as an iconic symbol of British history, offering visitors a captivating journey through centuries of royal heritage, political intrigue, and architectural grandeur. Its imposing presence on the banks of the River Thames and its fascinating stories make it a must-visit destination for tourists from all around the world.

Throughout this travel guide, we have explored the rich history and notable features of the Tower of London. From its humble beginnings as a defensive fortress to its transformation into a royal palace and a place of imprisonment, the Tower has witnessed and played a significant role in shaping the course of British history. Walking through its ancient walls, one can almost feel the echoes of the past, transporting them to a time when kings and queens ruled with absolute power.

The Tower's remarkable architecture is another highlight that adds to its allure. The White Tower, with its imposing presence and distinctive Norman design, showcases the grandeur of medieval construction. The stunning Crown Jewels, housed within the Jewel House, are a testament to the craftsmanship and opulence of the British monarchy. The iconic Tower Bridge, adjacent to the Tower of London, is a marvel of engineering and a prominent symbol of London itself.

Visiting the Tower of London provides a unique opportunity to delve into the lives of the famous and infamous figures who once inhabited its walls. From Anne Boleyn and Sir Walter Raleigh to Guy Fawkes and the Princes in the Tower, the Tower's history is intertwined with tales of political intrigue, betrayal, and tragic endings. The Yeoman Warders, or Beefeaters, who serve as guides, add a touch of authenticity to the experience with their colorful uniforms and wealth of knowledge.

Moreover, the Tower offers a range of engaging exhibits and activities that cater to diverse interests. Whether it's exploring the Royal Armories, discovering the medieval Torture at the Tower exhibition, or witnessing the ceremonial changing of the guard, there is something for everyone. The Tower also hosts exciting events throughout the year, such as reenactments, exhibitions, and seasonal festivities, ensuring that each visit is a unique and immersive experience.

Beyond its historical significance, the Tower of London is a vibrant cultural hub that attracts millions of visitors annually. Its riverside location provides breathtaking views of the city skyline, creating a picturesque backdrop for memorable photographs. The Tower's surrounding area, including the nearby St. Katharine Docks and the vibrant Borough Market, offers a multitude of dining and shopping options, allowing visitors to continue their exploration of London's diverse offerings.

In summary, the Tower of London is a treasure trove of history, culture, and architectural splendor. A visit to this iconic landmark is an opportunity to immerse oneself in the captivating stories of kings and queens, experience the majesty of centuries-old structures, and connect with the rich tapestry of British heritage. Whether you are a history enthusiast, an architecture admirer, or simply a traveler seeking an unforgettable experience, the Tower of London is a destination that should not be missed. Embark on a journey through time and unlock the secrets of this formidable fortress, and you will leave with a deeper appreciation for the legacy it holds and the indelible mark it has left on the pages of history.

Printed in Great Britain
by Amazon